The Autumn
Balloon

The Autumn Balloon

A Memoir

Kenny Porpora

GRAND CENTRAL
PUBLISHING

NEW YORK   BOSTON

Copyright © 2015 by Kenneth Porpora
All rights reserved. In accordance with the U.S. Copyright Act of 1976, the scanning, uploading, and electronic sharing of any part of this book without the permission of the publisher constitute unlawful piracy and theft of the author's intellectual property. If you would like to use material from the book (other than for review purposes), prior written permission must be obtained by contacting the publisher at permissions@hbgusa.com. Thank you for your support of the author's rights.

Grand Central Publishing
Hachette Book Group
1290 Avenue of the Americas
New York, NY 10104

www.HachetteBookGroup.com

Printed in the United States of America

RRD-C

First Edition: February 2015
10 9 8 7 6 5 4 3 2 1

Grand Central Publishing is a division of Hachette Book Group, Inc.
The Grand Central Publishing name and logo is a trademark of Hachette Book Group, Inc.

The Hachette Speakers Bureau provides a wide range of authors for speaking events. To find out more, go to www.hachettespeakersbureau.com or call (866) 376-6591.

The publisher is not responsible for websites (or their content) that are not owned by the publisher.

Library of Congress Cataloging-in-Publication Data

Porpora, Kenny.
     The autumn balloon / Kenny Porpora. — First edition.
        pages cm
     Summary: "Every autumn, Kenny Porpora would watch his heartbroken mother scribble messages on balloons and release them into the sky above Long Island, one for each family member they'd lost to addiction. As the number of balloons grew, his mother fell deeper into alcoholism, drinking away her sorrows every night in front of the television, where her love of Regis Philbin provided a respite from the sadness around her. When their house was foreclosed upon, Kenny's mother absconded with him and his beloved dog and fled for the Arizona desert, joining her heroin-addicted brother on a quixotic search for a better life. What followed was an outlaw adolescence spent in constant upheaval surrounded by bizarre characters and drug-addicted souls. In the wake of unspeakable loss, Kenny convinced a college to take a chance on him, and turned to the mentors, writers, and poets he found to rebuild the family he lost, and eventually graduated from the Ivy League with a new life. Porpora's memoir is the story of a deeply dysfunctional but loving family, and follows his life from the chaos of his youth to his triumphs in the Ivy League. At times darkly comic, at times elegiac, The Autumn Balloon is a beautifully written testament to the irreplaceable bonds of family, even under the most trying circumstances, and one that marks the debut of an exciting new writer"—Provided by publisher.
        ISBN 978-1-4555-4516-2 (hardback) — ISBN 978-1-4555-4515-5 (ebook) — ISBN (invalid) 978-1-4789-8331-6 (audio download)   1. Porpora, Kenny.   2. Porpora, Kenny—Childhood and youth.   3. Porpora, Kenny—Family.   4. Young men—United States—Biography.   5. College graduates—United States—Biography.   6. Children of alcoholics—United States—Biography.   7. Dysfunctional families—United States.   8. Alcoholics—Family relationships—United States.   9. Drug addicts—Family relationships—United States.   I. Title.
     CT275.P68194A3 2015
     305.242'10973—dc23
                                                                                            2014015983

For my mother.

The Autumn
Balloon

prologue

Times Square at rush hour. It's late spring.

Mobs of strangers and car honks, cops on horses and speeding cabs, hustlers handing out coupons for comedy shows and smiling Asian tourists and bike messengers running streetlights and men seated in front of easels sketching caricatures. I rush through, slipping sideways between teenagers flashing peace signs as they pose for the camera, and cut across the streets, push through the revolving glass doors of the Olive Garden, glide into the packed lobby, elbow my way to the escalator to the second floor, where casino neon intrudes through glass walls. From the center of this packed dining room, I look for her. And then I see my mother, sitting by herself in the corner.

I still call her Mommy and don't care who hears me so I yell for her and she turns and looks and waves me over. I'm wearing a suit with a turquoise graduation gown thrown over my shoulder and a matching turquoise cap in my hand.

She tells me my brother's on his way. She asks to see my

diploma, holds it in her hands and smiles, reads it out loud before handing it back to me, and I hold it tightly on my lap, this piece of paper, the proof they won't find me dead on a couch on my thirty-eighth birthday or in some basement bathtub with my eyes wide and lifeless or alone in the bed I slept in as a child with a Baggie of white powder under my mattress.

We talk about nothing, school and the city, then she starts telling me stories about her job at the school cafeteria and the people she serves, the motherfucker in the turban who calls her Kim no matter how many times she tells him her name and the woman she sees on Thursday who wears a duct-tape mask and sings Motown hits.

My brother, Steve, arrives, asks to see my diploma, too.

Our waiter interrupts to ask us if we're ready to order. My mother tells him that I just graduated from Columbia. Wow, he says. Congrats, dude. I put my head down. She's got proud, wide eyes. Tells him it's in the Ivy League. He says he knows. He asks us again if we're ready to order. We're still waiting on a few people, we tell him.

My professor arrives. His name is Ted, an older, graying man with a warm smile and soft midwestern twang to his voice. His ears jut out from the side of his head like windblown flaps. He's a recovered addict, thirty years sober, with a heaviness under his eyes and a PhD from the University of Nebraska. We met in a school elevator, and he could tell from the way I spoke that we had some sadness in common. He befriended me, listened to my stories, and shared some of his own. And then he helped me get my first job out of college.

"Hello, Mr. Ted," my mother says.

She shakes his hand and introduces herself. Ted was in the same fraternity as my brother, and when he shakes his hand, he asks him a secret question whose answer only members are allowed to know. My brother, caught off guard, blushes and thinks for a minute before answering.

"Kenny," Ted says, "when you told me we were having dinner at the Olive Garden, I seriously thought you were kidding..."

He likes to make fun of me for loving the Olive Garden.

My brother's best friend, Chris, arrives next, wearing an overcoat and a newsboy cap. He apologizes for being late. Hugs my mother hello. Shakes Ted's hand. He reminds me of my uncle. Makes me laugh the same way he did. Chris is ten years sober. He met my brother in a fraternity in northern Arizona where he got hazed for not drinking. He was the first person I ever met who quit drugs without any help.

My mother's telling a story about me as a little boy.

"I'm in the kitchen making breakfast and Kenneth comes out of his bedroom, five years old, bushy hair, and dressed up like the Joker. He told me he wouldn't go to school unless he could dress like the Joker, so I said fine. He had the white face paint, the big red lips, the green hair, purple jacket, little Velcro shoes..."

"This story explains so much," my brother says.

Everybody laughs. My mother goes on.

"He was such a little toughie. He'd come out of his room, thinking nothing of it, and say, 'Can you hear me talking to myself in my room?' And I'd be in the kitchen making breakfast and say, 'Yeah,' and he'd shrug and say, 'I'm just reciting dialogue.'"

The table laughs.

"I used to press my ear against the door and listen to him recite the lines. 'And where is the Batman? He's at home washing his tights!' And I'd wave his father over and we'd both press our ears against the door and listen. He memorized the whole movie. Used to make his brother act out scenes when he got back from school. I still have the tapes. I should've sent those tapes to Regis."

"And how long did you dress up like the Joker?" Ted asks.

"Until he was seventeen," my brother says with a laugh.

Chris laughs. "Yeah, till last semester..."

"He actually went to his graduation dressed as the Joker," my brother says.

In the morning my mother and I drive into our old neighborhood on Long Island to see our old house. We haven't seen it in years. A dozen balloons squeak and rub together in the backseat. The old video store is now a Dunkin' Donuts; our favorite pizza place is a gas station. We turn right onto Udall Road and pull onto our block. She parks her rental car on the other side of the road from our old house. There are new cars in the driveway. A little girl plays in the grass. The new owners have painted it, fixed it up a bit, installed a new fence. It doesn't look like ours anymore.

We drive to the ballpark in Massapequa where I once played Little League, and I grab the balloons out of the backseat. There's a sad jungle gym with a slide and monkey bars and a tire held up by chains; there's a neglected baseball diamond surrounded by brown grass and a rusted fence behind the catcher's box. There are some metal bleachers for parents to sit on to watch their children play.

"I wanna get back in time for *Days of Our Lives*," my mother says.

She likes to write messages on balloons and send them to

the sky. She takes out a black Magic Marker and starts writing on the dozen or so balloons, one for each member of our family who died. She doesn't think she can write well and asks me not to read her notes.

She likes to think they'll soar all the way to heaven. I think she knows they end up tangled in power lines or deflated in a pile of orange leaves in someone's backyard miles away, but I can never bring myself to say that to her. I've often wondered what they must think, those people who find our balloons. I've wondered if they read the messages and understand what they mean.

I remember watching those balloons as a little boy, each fall, wondering if someday I, too, would be nothing but a balloon in the sky, soaring toward the sun until I began to fall slowly back to earth and into the hands of a stranger.

"You know, it's a real shame," she says. Her eyes are covered by sunglasses, but I can tell she's crying. "Stupid assholes, all of them, with their drugs. Selfish. Very fuckin' selfish. Let's just get this over with."

My mother lets go of the balloons, and we watch them rocket upward too quickly until they become little floating dots. And then they disappear.

"Isn't that spooky?" she asks. "The way they took off so fast?"

We get into our car. She tells me I have a lot of good people around me, that I should be proud. And I say I am. And we drive out of this park and out of this town and onto the highway and away from this place.

PART ONE

chapter 1

A small, dark house somewhere on Long Island.

It's night.

My mother is drunk in her chair with an empty glass in her hands.

She mutters to herself in a low voice too sad to be a whisper. I'm watching her drink herself to sleep in front of a television set, just as I have every night since she lost her sister Gina, the one she loved the most, the one she had a secret language with. My mother is heavyset, and the red splotches on her face make her look like a sunburned child. Her head is bowed, and her face is relaxed, so her jowls hang loosely. She isn't quite awake but not asleep, either. She never really sleeps, just drifts in and out of consciousness.

There was a fight earlier. The floor is covered in shards of broken glass and ceramic plates and a little bit of blood. The phone hangs off the hook, and the dial tone pulses down the hallway. There is a foreclosure sticker in the window. Soon the windows will be boarded up and the doors chained. I don't know where we'll go, but for now, this is home.

My mother stirs in her chair and awakens to a rerun of *Cheers*. She is not pleased.

"Kenneth, what the fuck is this bullshit on the TV?"

She speaks with a perfect slur, angry and biting.

"It's *Cheers*," I tell her regretfully. "Your show is over."

"Where the fuck are we? Why is the *goddamn* television still on?"

"You fell asleep with it on."

She mocks my voice back to me. "You fell asleep with it on."

The television is blaring. It's the episode where Frasier and Norm debate the validity of Freud.

"Look at this bald asshole," she says, sipping from her glass. She's not impressed with Dr. Frasier Crane and she tells me so; except she doesn't call him Frasier, she calls him "that little sissy faggot man."

"I am so sick of grown men acting like assholes, I'm very sorry." She takes a sip. "Be a fucking man. My brother isn't a man. Your father isn't a man. You aren't a man. You're all a bunch of little faggot boys, like Frasier."

She takes another sip.

Cheers always pisses her off, and I should've known better and changed the channel before she woke. I grab the *TV Guide* from on top of the television to see what's on next. It's *M*A*S*H*. My heart sinks.

She fucking hates *M*A*S*H*.

My seventy-year-old father's been arrested again. There was a fight over a phone bill that turned quickly into a war of cursing and lamp throwing, my mother with a knife and my father pinning her hands down, screaming in her face, calling her dead sister a drunk, a junkie, and telling her she's going to drink herself to death the same way. And when he let her up, my mother, wasted and crying, punched herself in the arms until they bruised a deep purple, then called the police and told them my father hit her. He was charged with domestic violence and handcuffed on our front lawn wearing his baggy old-man briefs and black socks and an oversize shirt that made him look pantsless. They read him his rights and asked him to watch his head as they put him in the backseat of the cop car and drove him away. Our neighbors watched from their porches, their faces lit by red and blue police lights. I watched from my bedroom window.

It's a commercial, and my mother's glass is empty, so she gets up and stumbles toward our small kitchen, which is just a hot plate and a microwave and a small refrigerator. Ice cubes clink in the glass, and she fills it halfway with orange juice. She goes down the hall and into the bathroom, where she's hidden the vodka under the sink. She emerges in her nightgown, wielding a full glass.

"What the fuck are you looking at?"

I don't answer.

"You looking at my glass? Like your father? Mr. Judgmental. Mr. *I'm-so-fucking-important*. Why don't you go get a job and be a man? Why don't you get a job as a priest, so you can be a judgmental prick *and* fuck little boys?"

She makes herself laugh with that one and starts to write it down on a pad but immediately forgets exactly how she worded it.

"Kenneth, what did I just say? How did I *say* it, goddamn it?" I tell her, and she laughs again, almost surprised.

She is drinking herself to death.

I write in my notebook, stories and doodles and lists of my favorite cartoon characters, and wonder what will happen if she dies.

Her skin is warm, and she smells like alcohol.

"You're a little faggot, Frasier!" She's seated back in front of the TV, shouting now. "You're a nothing little man, and your skinny little nothing wife probably knows you're a fuckin' fag."

She nods in and out of consciousness, muttering some nonsense to herself. Soft, painful sounds with no shape.

"I don't wanna be here anymore," she says. "I just wanna go away."

"Don't say that," I say.

"I don't think I'm gonna be here much longer," she whispers, speaking to no one.

It's just after midnight. The *M*A*S*H* theme song is playing over the end credits. I kiss her and walk to my room. She stays in the dark living room, dreaming of her sister, the television glowing on her face. In the morning she'll hide the empty bottles outside behind the shed before waking me up for second grade.

By 9:00 a.m. my mother is alert and happy, drinking coffee and watching *Live! with Regis and Kathie Lee*. She loves Regis.

"You want some eggs?" she asks when I get out of bed.

"Sure."

"You want the kind where I cut the hole in the bread?"

"Okay."

She's still talking to me as I go into the bathroom and close the door.

"Your friend is gonna be on *Regis* later," she announces.

"My friend?"

"Yeah, the Riddler...not the Riddler, c'mon, who's the one? C'mon. Jack..."

"Jack Nicholson?"

"Yeah. He's gonna be on."

"Why is he my friend?"

"I don't know. You love *Batman*."

I do love *Batman*.

She is smiling this morning. She has a pretty face and a warm smile.

"You should really send some of your stories to Regis."

She always tells me to send anything I write to Regis Philbin. I don't know why. She thinks Regis is the sweetest man in the world. She tells me the story again of how Regis worked his way up from the mailroom to become the host of the show.

Kathie Lee is on vacation, so Regis's wife is the guest host. My mother despises her.

"I have no idea what he sees in this woman, I'm very sorry. She is so blah. And she can't sing for shit." She then tells me a story about how Regis's wife won't let him eat grape jelly and crackers in bed. I have no idea how she knows this. Some mornings she'll tell me Regis reminds her of my father. And then she'll become quiet and change the subject.

Her brother, my uncle Carter, is sitting at our table. He's just back from rehab, learning karate as part of his effort to stay sober. When he first got out, my mother took us to meet him at Dunkin' Donuts, and there he was, standing at the counter, ordering a Boston Kreme in flip-flops and a karate *gi*. Carter grew up a chubby little boy with a fear of needles. He was a runaway at fifteen and a criminal at sixteen and a heroin addict by twenty. He's now in his early thirties, tall and handsome, with a Tom Selleck mustache and dark brown hair cut into a mullet. He wears the karate *gi* pretty much everywhere he goes. He lives with their mother in Amityville and came over this morning to make sure my father didn't come back.

They're showing dogs from the North Shore Animal League on *Regis* this morning. One dog is white and fluffy with a teddy-bear face and a waggedy tail. Her name is Joy, but to me she looks more like a Wozels, so I call her Wozels and move closer to the television. My mother thinks she's adorable until she finds out the dog was named after Regis's wife. The woman from the animal shelter is talking about the dogs, but Joy Philbin interrupts and manages to plug her new Christmas album.

"Oh, shut the fuck up, Joy, nobody cares," my mother says from the kitchen. "She's even worse than Kathie Lee," she says. She asks me if I've ever seen Cody Gifford, Kathie Lee's son. I don't answer, just stare at the little white doggy on TV and watch her tilt her curious head and laugh at her perky ears. I love her.

"He's really nothing special," my mother says. "So he memorized a song at four years old? So what? So do all kids. He sounds like a pretentious asshole if you ask me."

She tells me I should show Regis how I've memorized all the lines to *Batman*.

The dog is quiet and shy and stands away from the others, not barking, just waiting for somebody to pet her and hold her. Regis finally asks about Joy, and the woman from the animal shelter says her family couldn't take care of her anymore, says she needs a new home. I call my mother, who's still angry at Kathie Lee in the kitchen.

"And she's way too fuckin' skinny..."

"Mom? Come here," I yell.

"What is she, a size zero? What is wrong with these men who want these women with little-boy bodies?"

"Mommy, quick..."

"What is it?"

She comes into the room, and I point at the TV.

"I know, Kenneth, I saw her. Very cute, I said." She goes back into the kitchen. The segment ends, and they take a commercial break and return with musical guests Boyz II Men.

My uncle lights a cigarette. His arms are scarred with tracks, dried bubbly skin that looks like burned marshmallows. The smoke fills our living room. My mother puts a plate of eggs and a cup of coffee in front of him.

"You should've heard Regis this morning," she says to him. "He was talking about Motown." My uncle likes to pretend he's the lead singer of a Motown group, usually when he's drunk at our house, hammering his drumsticks on the table and singing along to the radio.

"And I recorded Bruce Willis for you," she said. "He was on my morning show. He's a sweetheart. Did you know he plays harmonica?"

"Uncle Carter, you should've seen this doggy that was on before," I say. "So cute, with a little tongue and fluffy face. Her name was Joy, but if she was mine I'd call her Wozels."

"I saw her," he says and looks at my mother. He asks me where I got the name Wozels. I shrug and say I don't know, she just looks like a Wozels to me. We finish our breakfast, and he tells me he'll take me to school. My mother zips up my backpack and hands me my Dick Tracy lunch box.

"Your prick father is gonna pick you up from school today," she tells me. "Make sure he has you back by five."

I nod.

She starts making fun of my father for lying about his age, for the way he dyes his hair black with cheap shoe polish, and for telling people he's fifty-four when he's really seventy. My uncle laughs at him, too, calls him pathetic and shakes his head, blowing cigarette smoke out of the side of his mouth before dabbing the cigarette out into an ashtray.

I get sad on the drive to school, so my uncle tries to distract me with a silly story. He pulls up right to the front door of the school and kisses me good-bye. He reminds me my father is going to be picking me up. I nod and close the car door and walk to my classroom.

Second grade is a lonely place for me. My hair is shaggy, and I wear a small leather jacket and Velcro shoes and a clip-on earring that makes me feel older. I stay mostly to myself except for when I talk to an obese Hispanic girl named Melinda, who suffers from a violent lisp. She has a crush on me. Sometimes we eat lunch together, and sometimes my teachers force the other kids to let me sit with them in the cafeteria. Some days my mother packs me chocolate chip cookies with rainbow sprinkles along with my lunch, and this is the highlight of my day. She writes me little notes every day and hides them in my lunch box, and when I find them, I go to where it's quiet and read them. Usually I eat alone and wander the playground and watch the older kids play handball against the brick school walls.

My father is waiting outside the school for me today in his beat-up Volvo, which I've nicknamed Bobby. I run out to meet him. He asks me where my brother is, and I tell him he's down the block at a friend's house. We ride in Bobby together down the hilly roads, up and down, like when I was a baby. The inside of Bobby is covered in dried oil, splattered on the ceiling, the seats, the doors, the rugs, and nobody seems to know why. The toxic smell seeps into our clothes, our hair, our skin.

We arrive at the baseball park and sit side by side on Bobby's rusted bumper and look out onto the neglected field. I eat the ham sandwich he made me, which tastes a bit like oil, and drink lemonade out of an old Clorox bottle, since my father doesn't like to waste anything. I need two hands to hold the bottle to my lips, and still some drips down my chin. He eats fast, stuffing his sandwich into his mouth and forcing the rest in with his fingers. He is crying and eating and talking at the same time.

"I'm not fifty-four," he tells me. He looks gray and broken. "I'm old, kiddo. I'm an old man. And I don't know how many years I have left."

I know he's old, and I know he's going to die soon. Some days, when he drops me off at school, I get out of the car and try to memorize his face.

"I know you're old," I tell him. "Mommy tells us you're old all the time. She calls you the old prick when you're not around."

"I can't keep fighting and getting arrested and fighting and crying," he says. "I'm just too old."

He's been living some nights with us and some nights with his last living brother, who chain-smokes and watches *Star Trek*. He tells me he found a basement apartment a few blocks away and asks me if I'd like to live with him. I say that I would. He says he's going to hire a lawyer to fight for full custody. He tells me there's a possibility that my brother and I will be separated from each other, and I nod and try not to cry. He asks me whose idea the clip-on earring was, and I tell him it was mine. I think about being away from my mother, and I get sad. She needs me.

The TV is on with no sound. Our living room is dark and mostly empty. My brother is asleep in his room. My mother is drunk again. She calls my name from the bathroom once and then again, her voice muddled.

I walk down our half-lit hallway, past the fist-size holes in the walls, past the crooked framed baby pictures of my brother and me, to where the bathroom door is cracked open. I stand and speak into the slight opening.

"Mommy?"

She speaks slowly, every word an effort.

"Kenneth...

"...can you come in here?...

"...I need you..."

I push the bathroom door open. My mother sits on the edge of the toilet, her head hanging heavy over her lap, her nightgown pulled up high enough for me to see her brown pubic hair.

"Are you okay?" I ask.

"Come in here, goddamn it!"

I stand close and ask her what she needs. My bare feet are cold on the cracked blue tile. Light from the moon pours in through a small window above our shower.

"Where the fuck am I?" she asks me.

I stand in front of her and don't answer.

"Your aunt Gina loved you, you know. Do you know that?"

"Yes," I say.

Her sister Gina left home at eighteen and had two children

with some black guy before she was disavowed by the family and told never to bring her nigger children around. She had been drinking herself to death for years, drinking until she vomited so intensely that she burst the capillaries in her face. The jerking of her head forced her mouth to smash into the cold ceramic toilet seat, breaking her four front teeth. She spit bits of tooth and blood and bitten tongue onto the floor and kept vomiting until she fell asleep on the cool tile. For days afterward she walked around with black eyes, looking like a beaten raccoon. Another fit of violent puking led to a brain aneurysm, and she died with her head propped up on the toilet seat. Her children went to live with their father and, later, some friends.

"She was so happy at the hospital when you were born. And she waited up with your brother..."

She tries to cry, to speak, and can't do either.

"...and when the doctors told her you were a boy, she shouted, 'It's a boy!' and your brother leaped into her arms."

Her tears drop onto her thigh.

"And...

"...she used to hold you...

"...and play with your little toes."

Her voice is fading away. She is fading away. I watch her struggle to keep herself on the toilet. She starts to hum a song, half sings the words, then begins to mutter to herself, something I can't understand, and her head falls again.

And then, with a sudden burst of anger, "Goddamn it! Help me!"

"How?" I ask in a small voice.

She's quiet for a moment.

"Kenneth?"

I tell her I'm still there. Ask her again what she needs.

"Can you wipe me?"

Her voice is pathetic, her arms limp at her sides. I touch her shoulder. I love her.

"I need you to wipe me," she says again, then a hiccup jolts through her frame.

"Okay," I say.

I reach for the toilet paper and wind it around my hand and tear it.

"Can you sit up?"

"She was thirty-five fucking years old, goddamn it!"

"Mommy, can you sit up?"

She can't.

I reach my hand into the toilet, underneath her, our faces close enough for me to feel the heat from her red cheeks, to feel the warm wetness of the tears on her face, to smell the sharpness of the vodka on her breath. I can feel the heat of her shit through the tissue on my hand.

"I love you, baby boy," she says.

"I know you do."

"You're like me," she says. "You care about people. I care about people. I care too goddamn much."

I reach for more toilet paper, ball it up in my palm, and wipe her again.

"Don't let people take advantage of you," she says. "You understand me? You're a very special boy."

"Okay," I say.

I throw the tissue in the water and flush the toilet.

"You're good."

"Grab my arm," she says. "I need help getting up."

I help her walk out of the bathroom, down the hall, and

into the living room, where she collapses into her chair. She wants to fall asleep in the chair, she says. She's afraid if she lies down in bed she won't wake up.

We sit together in the smoking section of a diner off Jericho Turnpike, my mother, my uncle, my brother, and me. My uncle is smoking, dabbing his ash onto a plate. He is not in his *gi*. He has a briefcase next to him in the booth.

"So your fucking prick father served me with papers today," my mother says. The waitress comes around, and I order French toast. My brother orders an omelet.

"What's in the briefcase?" I ask my uncle, half ignoring my mother.

"I'm talking, Kenneth," my mother says. "The old prick wants custody, and if he wins, we won't see each other anymore. Is that what you want?"

I shake my head. My brother shakes his head.

"Then you better tell the caseworker you want to live with me, okay?"

My brother asks where we're going to go once the house is foreclosed on. He's eleven and smarter than I am. He reads John Grisham.

"We'll be fine," she says. "I'll figure it out."

My uncle taps his briefcase and smiles. He says he's got the answer to our problems inside.

"Carter, not now with the bullshit, okay?"

The waitress drops off four glasses of water and disappears.

"What's in it?" I ask again.

He sets the briefcase on the table and unsnaps it, raises the lid slowly. Inside is a yellowed newspaper.

"This is the original copy of the *Amityville Record* from

the day after the *Amityville Horror* murders took place," he says.

"What does that mean?" my brother asks.

"It means I'm rich," he says. "It means I have a connection in Arizona who knows a guy who's willing to pay a fortune for this."

My brother asks him how much, and my uncle says, "Let's just say the number had six zeroes after it."

He smiles and takes a drag of his cigarette. My mother's family grew up with the boy who murdered his entire family and whose life inspired *The Amityville Horror.*

"I can't just take the kids out of school and go on some fuckin' wild-goose chase," my mother says.

"It's not a goddamn wild-goose chase," he growls. "It's a gold mine."

"Stephen has friends here, Carter," she says. "We can't just pick up and move."

Our food comes. I use too much syrup, and my brother makes fun of me. He asks me why I'm wearing a clip-on earring and laughs and I tell him to shut up. '

"You look gay," he says.

"Knock it the fuck off with that," my mother says. "Stop calling your brother gay. You're gonna turn him gay if you keep saying it."

We ride together in silence to a motel. My uncle is staying there tonight with a friend, someone we don't know.

He gets out and slams the door. "If you change your mind about Arizona, let me know. You're gonna regret not getting in on this," he says and pats his briefcase.

My mother tells him to say a prayer for Gina. He says he will. He walks up the concrete steps of the motel, and we drive away, our tires crunching on pavement, down Sunrise Highway and back to our house.

I sit alone in the back of my school bus and daydream, counting the stops. Three more until I'm home. The bus is pretty empty, but up ahead, a few kids sit together and laugh and talk about X-Men. I love X-Men, but they're getting details wrong and it takes everything I have not to walk up the aisle and correct them. I have a quick fantasy where I tap one of them on the shoulder and let him know that Wolverine is, in fact, not Magneto's son.

The bus pulls up to the corner I recognize, the one with the graffitied stop sign. I walk past the group of kids to exit the bus and say nothing. I walk the half mile from the bus stop to our house. I always half expect to see cop cars out front, but it's quiet today. I go inside my house and throw my backpack on the stairs. *X-Men* is coming on soon, and I go to the refrigerator to find a Capri Sun. My mother comes into the kitchen. She looks pretty today, her hair up in barrettes.

"Hi, baby boy, how was school?"

"Good," I say. "I did a word search."

Word search is my favorite.

"You did?" She kisses my cheek, and I tell her I'm going to watch some cartoons.

"Actually," she says, "could you go in your room and grab me some papers off the desk?"

I'm immediately suspicious.

"What papers?"

"Just some court papers," she says.

I set down my Capri Sun and head down the hallway to my room. I open the door, and the white doggy from *Regis and*

Kathie Lee jumps off my bed and into my arms. She is soft and fluffy and even more adorable in real life. She climbs all over me, excited, and hair falls over her brown eyes and she licks my face with her pink tongue and I hug her. She is my best friend.

"Isn't she precious?" my mother shouts. She is smiling and taking photos.

I am giggling as the dog licks my face.

"She's the one from *Regis and Kathie Lee*!" she tells me. I tell her I know. The dog rolls onto her back, and I pet her belly. She doesn't bark. She is sweet and gentle. She jumps up onto the couch and starts sniffing around.

"I'm going to name her Wozels," I say, then call her name and pat my lap.

My mother tells me the story about how she got Wozels while I roll around on the floor with the dog, happier than I've ever been. Wozels jumps up on the dining room table and lies down, her tail wagging. My mother tries to get angry, but she can't. Wozels is too silly. We both laugh, and Wozels jumps down and back into my arms.

"I went down to the shelter this morning right after I dropped you off at school," she says. "The woman behind the front counter was a real nasty bitch. She told me Joy had already been adopted. You shoulda heard her tone…"

Wozels's tail is wagging, thumping against the carpet. Her ears are perky. She is perfect to me.

"So I said, 'Oh, darn it,' and started looking around and sure enough, there she was, there was Joy-Joy, sound asleep in her cage, as sweet as can be…"

I pick Wozels up and brush her fur from her eyes. I kiss her snout, and she licks my face.

"And then when I'm filling out the paperwork she says to

me, she says, 'What color is she?' I said, 'What color is she? What color do you think she is? She's white, you stupid bitch!' Look at her! Isn't she white, Kenneth? Tell me she's not white . . ."

"She's white," I say.

Her coat is white and soft and her ears are floppy and she's got big, dopey paws and she runs around our living room.

"Can Wozels sleep in my room?" I ask.

"Maybe. We'll see."

I kiss my mother on the cheek. She hugs me close, happy to see me so happy.

"What about when I go visit Daddy? Can I bring her?"

"No," she says sharply. "You know what, Kenneth? Stop bringing up the old prick's name! Okay? He'll probably let her out. You want her to run away?"

"No."

"Go play with your dog in your room," she says. "My soaps are coming on."

I pick Wozels up.

"Don't put your face in hers. She'll bite your face off, and I don't feel like rushing you to the hospital."

She makes herself a drink and puts her feet up on the ottoman. I take Wozels into my room and close the door, and I watch her sniff around my blankets, paw at them, poke her snout under the bed, and we play together until it's time for bed. It'll be a few days before the marshal comes banging on the front door, telling us to get out.

Wozels jumps on my bed and rests her chin and snout down on my mattress. I kneel down beside her.

"Hello," I say. "It's very nice to meet you."

I rest my head beside hers and close my eyes.

chapter 2

A light rain falls. The newly dawned sun is already lost behind clouds. In the distance, a red stoplight reflects off the wet street.

The court decided my brother would live with my father and I would live with my mother, and on Saturdays my father would get a three-hour visitation. I'm buckled into the backseat of Bobby, daydreaming. My brother is in the passenger seat. My father is driving, humming an old love song, tapping the steering wheel. Now and then my clip-on earring starts to make my ear itch, so I switch it to my other ear. I have a photograph of Wozels in my hand. Whenever I'm not with her, I carry it with me. My father pulls up to a dilapidated one-story house with toys in the yard, an oil-stained driveway, and an old car propped up on cinder blocks. Blankets hung like curtains on the windows. My father rents the basement.

We walk across the grass. Before he knocks on the door, he reminds us that his landlady, Linda, is in a wheelchair and has only one leg. He asks us to be respectful. He also reminds us that she thinks he's fifty-four, not seventy, just in case she asks. She's very nice, he says. And she has a pet pig named Kevin.

He knocks.

Knocks again.

The door opens, and I hear a bassoon-like snort and see the pig's brown snout pressed up against the screen door.

"Oh, Kevin, goddamn it, get back," Linda says. "Sal, come get the goddamn pig, please."

There's a bit of a tussle, and the pig is detained, allowing Linda to open the wooden door fully.

"Louie?" she asks through the screen.

"Linda, hey, these are my boys."

She opens the screen door.

"Oh, let me get a look at you."

She is an obese woman with glasses and dull brown hair so long it would fall past her lower back if she were to stand. A blanket covers her lap, and I stare at her stump until my brother elbows me.

"Stevie!" she says and hugs my brother. My brother is tall for an eleven-year-old, still a bit chubby, with freckles and a close-cropped haircut. "How's the pitching?" she asks him, and he says it's going well.

"And you must be Kenny," she says. "Come here, darling."

She wheels toward me for a hug. She reeks of cigarettes. I hug her.

"Well, come on in out of the rain," she says, turning herself around and wheeling back into the house. We follow.

She tells us she made us some meat-loaf sandwiches, except she pronounces the word as "sangwiches."

My father tells me he's going to get our bags out of the trunk and run them downstairs. He asks my brother for help.

I wander alone through a squalid maze of old laundry, half-eaten plates of week-old spaghetti, bowls of overflowing cat food. The house is dark like a cave, shrouded in shadows, the only slivers of daylight sneaking in beneath doors. In the kitchen, I see tile stained with cat piss, beer cans, an ant-swarmed doughnut on the floor next to stacks of yellowed newspapers, old *Life* magazines, porno magazines, a VHS tape called *Smut City*, untied garbage bags piled to the sinking ceiling, burned spoons in the sink. If there's a kitchen table, I can't see it. Flies buzz over and around the spaghetti, the sink, the cans, the shit, the garbage.

I stand in the middle of it all, trying not to breathe in the smell of cat shit or pig shit or even human shit wafting in the air.

"Who are you?" asks a small voice.

I turn around and see a little girl with stringy blond hair and a dirty face. Her arms are covered in yellow and deep purple bruises, her legs are covered with welts. She's wearing a pink one-piece bathing suit, and she's barefoot.

"My name is Kenny. Who are you?"

"I'm Katie," she says. "Are you gonna live with us?"

I shake my head no, tell her my father moved into the basement.

"I thought he was your grandpa," she said.

"No," I say. "Everybody thinks that. He's my dad."

"How old is he?" she asks.

I freeze for a moment. Think.

"He's fifty-four," I say confidently and smile. "How old are you?"

She says she's nine.

"Linda's your mom?" I ask.

"My godmother. I stay here when my mom can't take care of me."

I nod my head. I understand her.

"Do you want to be friends?" she asks me. "We could play tag outside."

I say sure. "Sometimes I play manhunt with my brother and his friends, but that's a game for older kids. They let me play, though," I tell her, almost bragging.

She asks me how to play.

"There's two people," I say. "They stand on opposite sides of the block with boundaries keeping them apart. And the whole thing is, you have to cross their boundaries, and when you do you keep yourself hidden and try to get to their base before they get to yours. But it sucks because you never know if they're playing defense or offense, you know? So it's like, they could be hiding and waiting for you. And if they catch you they put you in jail."

"And then what happens?"

"And then you have to wait there alone until somebody from your team comes. I hate it because I always end up getting caught first and then waiting forever for somebody. And sometimes they never come and you're just waiting for no reason. And then you find out there's nobody left on your team to save you."

"And what then?"

I shrug.

"Then the game's over."

I hear Linda's bark from the other room, her voice quickly getting louder as she approaches.

"You like pro wrestling, Ken?"

I love pro wrestling.

She wheels up to me and hands me an unlabeled VHS tape.

"This is a classic," she says. "From my collection. You can't keep it, though. Make sure you bring it back, okay?"

I nod.

"We're gonna eat in the dining room. I cleared some space for us. Sal," she yells. "We're eating."

I walk up and stand next to my brother.

"Why are you standing so close to me?" he asks. "I can feel your gay arm touching me."

"Shut up. It's gross in here," I tell him. "I wanna go. I'm afraid to walk anywhere. And it stinks."

"I don't know what to do," he says. "We have to stay for now, so just relax. Try not to breathe."

We take our seats around the table, where she serves us meat-loaf sangwiches.

Sal, an older man with a full head and beard of curly gray hair, comes lumbering into the dining room in a dirty, mustard-stained T-shirt and boxer shorts. He kisses Katie on the head, sits beside me, and extends his hand. His knuckles have cuts on them.

"Sal," he says.

"Hi," I say. "I'm Kenny."

His hand is warm and rough. My brother shakes his hand next. He acknowledges my father with a nod.

"Meat-loaf sang again?" he asks his wife.

"I should waste it?"

"Ken, you and Katie should go play in the woods behind here, do kid shit. You know?"

I nod.

"Excited about coming to live with Dad for good?"

I nod. Look at my father. At my brother.

"Now's not a good time to talk about it," my father says. "The kids are gonna miss their mother."

"Your mother sounds sick to me," Sal says. He takes a big bite, chews sloppily.

I picture myself older, stronger, with a five o'clock shadow and an overcoat, coming into the living room while he sits in his boxer shorts watching pro wrestling. I tell him to stand up, and we square off, face-to-face.

"So you have a pig?" my brother asks.

"Isn't he darling?" Linda says. "He sleeps in bed with me."

"Hate that pig," Sal says.

I chew my meat loaf, wanting to throw up. The air is thick. My hands feel dirty.

I look at Sal's arm. The inside of his elbow joint looks tracked and red-dotted. Like my uncle's. My father is eating fast, telling Linda a story about how he's going to start singing again. Big-band-era songs at nursing homes.

"Well, I hope you boys decide to come stay here full-time," Linda says. "And Katie would love it, too, wouldn't you, Kate?"

Katie nods.

"I think somebody has a little crush, huh, Ken?" Sal says and nudges me. "Ain't Katie a cute girl?"

"Oh, God," my brother says with a groan.

"Katie always gets shy when she likes a boy," Sal says, laughing. "Ain't that right?"

It's quiet as everyone finishes their sandwiches.

"Well, we better do it," my father says and begins to stand. I thank Linda for the wrestling tape. She tells me again not to lose it.

"Ken, a pleasure," Sal says, and gruffly shakes my hand again.

"Steve-O, good to see ya again."

Linda wheels ahead of us. The pig wails from the other room. The door from the kitchen leads to the basement. She opens it for us and wishes us a good night.

The basement is all tile, dark and mildewed, with a single naked lightbulb hanging from the ceiling. My father pulls a string, and a hard fluorescence lights the room.

"Man, that was some awful meat loaf," he says, taking off his jacket.

I follow him down the hall. He turns on the bathroom light. The bathtub is crusted with dirt and roaches, and I jump back into the hallway.

"Dad, there's bugs."

"Yeah, I gotta get somebody in here," he says, nonchalant, and turns on the faucet to wash his hands.

"They're gonna crawl on you while you sleep," my brother says with a laugh.

My father yells over the running water, "Don't go tellin' your mother about the bathtub. I'm getting someone in here. She'll have me in court in five minutes."

In the bedroom, I sit with my brother on the unmade bed.

"Where are you and Mommy living?" he asks me.

"In the car," I say. "Behind Dairy City. But she says we're going to get a place soon. How long are you going to stay here?"

He shrugs, then flicks my ear.

"Ow. You're such an asshole..."

I cover my mouth.

He looks at me wide-eyed.

"I didn't, I stopped myself..."

"Like I care if you say asshole," he says. "I say asshole all the time."

I get up and peek down the hall to see where my father is. He's humming in the kitchen. I look back at my brother.

"You do?"

"Yeah," he says. "I say fuck, too."

"What? Does Mommy know?"

"Because she never says fuck?"

Every time he says it I jump a little and peek again down the hallway.

"Try it," he says.

I shake my head no and clench my mouth closed.

"So gay."

"I am not."

"Then say it."

I stare at him, a standoff. He's smiling. I'm terrified.

And then I whisper, "Fuck?"

"Are you asking me?"

He leans in closer with his ear cocked toward me and smiles.

"Fuck," I say again, this time a little louder. It feels freeing.

He says it back to me, with more confidence, and a little attitude, "Fuck."

"Fuck," I say.

We're trading fucks now.

"Fuck."

"Fuck."

"Fuck."

I laugh harder every time he says it. I feel older, standing here with my brother, with my earring, saying fuck like it's no big deal.

"Fuck fuck fuck fuck fuck," I say, and he explodes into laughter. I laugh, too. I miss him being around.

"Kenny, come here," my father yells from down the hall. "We have to talk before your mother gets here to pick you up."

In the kitchen, he asks me to sit down at the creaky kitchen table in seats whose cushions are ripped, their yellow foam innards spilling out.

"I talked to Katz," he says. Katz is his lawyer. "And the courts want you to come live here with me full-time."

I think about my mother and try not to cry. I think about Wozels, and I try not to cry. I look at my brother, who's now standing behind me, and he looks back at me. He always knows.

"It's gonna be okay, though, Kenny," my brother says. "And you can come out with me and my friends and I'll teach you how to ride a bike."

"What about Wozels?" I ask my father.

"It's just a dog, kiddo."

I shake my head. She's my best friend.

"You can bring her here," my brother says.

"Here? With Kevin the pig? He'll eat her!"

"All right, calm down," my father says.

"Now, listen, don't you wanna see your dad every day?"

I look at him and nod. I love him.

"Your mother has some problems she has to work out," he says. "You got a nice place here, you can stay in your classes, and it'll be fine."

I look at my brother. He nods with a half smile.

I nod, too.

"When?" I ask.

"Starting next month," he says. "Three weeks from now. Your mother will drop you off just like she always does, except she won't pick you up."

I think about her being alone. I nod again. Keep nodding.
"Does she know yet?" I ask.

Yes, he says.

I am quiet again. I wonder why she didn't say anything to
me. I'm afraid if I speak I'll start to cry, so I stay silent.

"Don't we have fun together?" my father asks in a somber
voice. "We could have a catch every night in the backyard."

I smile at him.

Yes, I say. Of course we have fun.

Bay Shore is a lonely town with streetlights that hang on
wires. My mother's light-blue Colt is parked in the lot behind
some forgotten strip mall: a sad bar that reeks of spilled beer
with an out-of-date TV that only plays Mets games; a Chinese
restaurant named Chinese Restaurant; a stationery store; and
the place my mother buys her vodka. Our car has blankets and
pillows piled in the backseat and a water bowl for Wozels on
the floor. We've made it through the worst of winter, but the
car is cold at night, no matter how bundled we are. I haven't
asked her about my father being awarded custody yet.

It's midday, but under this permanently overcast sky, it
always seems like night. My mother's on a pay phone, pacing as
far as the cord will let her go. I walk Wozels in the weeds, her
small paws getting muddy from the puddles. She's a year old
and still curious about everything she sees. She looks under
cars for hiding cats and knows that balancing on her hind legs
and waving will get her whatever she wants. My mother heads
back toward us.

"That was Karen," she says. "I got the job!" She has a
pretty smile. The job is part-time, taking school pictures for
the yearbook of the preschool in Amityville where her friend

Karen works as a secretary. She went to high school with Karen, and they swam together, played softball. They hadn't spoken in more than ten years, but my mother looked her up in a phone book and asked if she could help. It's a chance for her to get enough money together to get a motel room, then maybe an apartment of our own.

It's night. We sleep. I hear a tapping just above my head, unsure if I'm dreaming or not. My mother snores. I peek my head out from under the blanket and look up at the window, where a black man with a hood covering most of his face is peering inside our car. We make eye contact. He stares at me, his eyes wide and wild. He motions for me to roll down my window. I can't move.

"Mom," I say softly. She's passed out. My father's old baseball bat lies beside her on the floor of the passenger side. There's a smaller bat on the floor nearer to me. The man is still there.

"Mom!" I shout, and she gasps awake.

"What is it? You okay?"

"Mom, there's a man at the window."

She turns to look. Sees him. Tells me to stay down. She reaches over slowly and grabs the handle of the bat. I reach down and grab the one near me. The man moves to the driver's side and bangs on the window.

"Go away—I called the cops!" she yells at him.

He pulls on the door handle. And again. Harder this time. Bangs the window.

"What do you want?" she yells.

He just stares at her. He seems mentally handicapped, unsure of what he wants, where he is.

"Are the keys in the ignition?" I ask her.

"Yes," she says.

"Just start the car and drive away."

She slowly lets go of the bat and quickly turns the key. The engine stutters, but it starts. The man is startled and backs away, but not before slapping the window and the hood of the car. My mother puts the car in reverse and speeds backwards, stops, shifts into drive, and tears out of the parking lot.

We head onto the highway, out of the town and into another. I let go of my bat. There is an unspoken pledge between the two of us, alone together on these streets: we are willing to protect each other at all costs. We park across the street from a police precinct. Neither of us goes back to sleep that night.

In the morning, we meet Karen at the preschool, and I help my mother carry out all the school's equipment that she'll need—an expensive camera, a soft light, and a heavy tripod—and load it into the backseat. The next few nights, we park overnight in the school lot. My mother takes me out of class for the day, and I wander the hallways and peek into classrooms while my mother works. Kids dressed in vests and khakis file into the hallway in straight lines and are led into the large cafeteria, where my mother has the camera set up. She's good with kids, knows how to get them to smile. For as long as I can remember, my mother has wanted to be a school-teacher. I watch her from the back of the cafeteria. She has them sit on a wooden block, has them tilt their heads. *Smile. Not too much. That's it. Just like that. And hold it.* Snaps the photo. She has hundreds of these to do.

Together, Wozels and I sit in the car. Nap. Wander around

outside. I talk to her often. She's a good listener. I try to teach her some new tricks, but she's more interested in the flurry of smells emanating from the nearby grass.

Two weeks later, my mother gets her first paycheck from the school. We go grocery shopping, picking up bread, peanut butter, jelly, pretzels, peanuts, cold cuts, vodka, orange juice, peanut M&M's. She proudly tells the checkout lady she's a photographer. Says how tired she is from working so hard. The clerk says she knows the feeling. My mother's been referred to another preschool to take some photos. We even have enough money to go to a movie, *The Mighty Ducks*, with Emilio Estevez. It's more than cool enough outside to leave Wozels in the car, and my mother and I sit together for a few hours, alone in the barely lit theater, and everything feels like it's going to be okay.

At night, my mother tells me she's going to hire a lawyer and fight to get custody back. She says she's going to show the courts she can take care of us.

The sun retreats behind clouds, and we take the back roads to our storage unit. We're six months behind in our payments. The Italian guy who operates the storage facility is named Giuseppe, but my mother calls him "that fucking guinea," and he says we have one more month to get the money together or he's going to auction off our belongings. Whatever remnants of our former life are still in existence are in that unit. My father's old clothing; his books and photographs. My old toys, baby clothes, baby teeth, schoolwork stuffed in backpacks. Boxes of dishes, silverware, Christmas ornaments. My mother has one month's payment in cash in an envelope.

The rows of storage units are identical. I sit with Wozels in front of our unit, my back resting against the heavy metal door, the combination lock pressing into my lower back. Wozels licks her paws. My mother pulls the car around. Gets out.

"He says he'll give us another month," she says. "Acted like he was doing us a fuckin' favor. I just handed him three hundred dollars. That's a lot of money."

She undoes the lock, and we pull the clattery door up together. In front of us, we see our old couch, mattresses, boxes piled to the concrete roof.

"Grab whatever you think you need for now," she tells me.

She helps me move around some heavy boxes, and I find one full of old Hulk comics I'd thought I'd lost. I rifle through them, pick out a few of my favorites, and put the box back on top of the heap.

"Want anything else?" she asks. "Your father's clarinet? His baseball glove?"

I shake my head. "I'll grab the rest when we come back."

It's a Wednesday night. We're driving around looking for a liquor store. We find one, and my mother pulls into the lot and tells me to wait in the car. Wozels has been in the car for hours and needs to go out. I hook her leash onto her collar and the two of us stroll behind the liquor store as I daydream. Wozels sniffs everything in sight, marks her territory. She loves it outside, but hasn't yet mastered the art of walking on a leash. She keeps getting her legs tangled, and I laugh and help untangle her just to watch her do it over again.

"Kenneth!" I hear a scream. "Goddamn it, no!"

Her scream is painful, familiar, and I feel it in my chest. And then in my stomach. I run with Wozels around to the front of the store. My mother is standing beside the car surrounded by broken glass. The back window is smashed. She's crying. Hysterical.

"They stole the goddamn camera!"

I stand, unable to move.

"Get in the fuckin' car, maybe we can find him."

I open the back door, and Wozels jumps in. I jump into the passenger seat. My mother peels out of the parking lot and speeds up and down the road. Her face is a dark red.

"I told you not to get out of the fucking car!" She's screaming so loud I can barely make out her words. "It was probably some nigger who's gonna sell it for crack! If I find the motherfucker I'm gonna kill him!"

We drive around the neighborhood.

Through parking lots.

Down back roads.

Into gas stations.

I run into stores and ask if anybody has seen anything. Nobody has. We drive to the pawn shop to ask them. They shake their heads no. We keep looking for hours, inside giant garbage bins in the back of supermarkets. We look everywhere.

It's just after midnight when she pulls over to the side of the road and stares straight ahead, her eyes furious and wide. Her teeth clenched. Her hands tight on the wheel. And then she breaks down and cries like a child, her face in her hands.

Rain patters softly on the roof of the car. My mother's on a pay phone, talking to her friend Karen, trying to explain how the camera was stolen, turning in small circles and asking her for another chance. She hangs up and rests against the side of the booth. I go to her. Karen can't help us. Our storage unit will be auctioned off. Our belongings. Everything we have. I put my hand on her shoulder. We stand together in the parking lot. Cars pass us by on the busy main road, their tires swooshing on the wet pavement, their headlights beaming and then vanishing.

chapter 3

The waiting room of the counseling center is pastel and tran-quil, with a CD of calming Native American flute music play-ing. The room smells sharply of pine needles from a plug-in air freshener.

My brother's reading an issue of *People* that has Princess Diana smiling on the cover. I stare up at a painting on the wall of a ragged woman with a small boy who looks almost too big to be sitting on her lap. I stand and look more closely at it. It's dark and distorted, blacks and greens and dark blues, but there's something beautiful about it. The door opens and our court-appointed counselor, Bruce, steps out. He is white-haired but still youthful, and he speaks gently.

"Boys, you can come on in."

We follow him into the small room and sit on classroom chairs. Bruce sits in front of us with his legs crossed and grabs a pad of paper. His pant leg is hiked up enough for me to see his patterned sock. He stares at me. Minutes pass. Long minutes.

"So Ken, last week we ended with you talking about a boy

in your gym class—Ethan, was it?—who was making fun of your X-Men underpants."

"Incredible Hulk," I say and nod.

"Any new developments?"

"Not really. I asked my dad for the plain white ones."

"And then he cried because he was scared he was growing up too fast," my brother says and smiles.

"I didn't cry."

My brother affects a British accent. "Father! I feel I am growing up much too fast!"

Bruce has no reaction. I stare daggers at my brother.

"And otherwise school is going well?"

I nod.

My brother and I have been living with my father full-time for the last couple of months, the three of us in Linda's basement apartment. My mother and Wozels moved back in with my grandmother. She's only allowed to see us once a month now, and the visits have to be supervised by a court-approved friend of my mother's from high school, who is there when my father drops us off and leaves right afterward.

Every week, before we go to counseling, my father tells us Bruce is going to try to trick us into giving him information about the roaches, the pet pig, Sal's collection of porn, Linda's chain-smoking, or Katie, who's always wandering the streets barefoot and alone. We answer cautiously.

"Any friends?" Bruce asks.

"Not really," I say.

"Why don't you tell Bruce about your new girlfriend, Katie," my brother says.

"She is not my girlfriend!" I say. "She's just some girl I play with sometimes."

"You became upset when your brother mentioned the possibility of her as your girlfriend," Bruce says softly.

"I didn't get upset."

The hour goes by slowly. My brother talks about his Little League team making the playoffs and the big game coming up.

"How has it been adjusting to life without Mom?" Bruce asks.

We're both quiet.

"Okay. We're going to have to stop now, but before we do, Ken, I noticed you staring at that painting outside."

I nod.

"Did you see something you liked about it?"

I shrug.

"It's a van Gogh."

"For real? I thought it kinda sucked."

Bruce smiles. "Well, it's not a real van Gogh. It's a reproduction. I actually found it at a garage sale out in Copiague. It's called *Mère et Enfant*. In French it means 'mother and child.'"

"Okay," I say.

"Does that change the meaning of it to you at all?"

"No," I say. "I don't think so."

We sit on the curb outside the counseling center and wait for our father to pick us up.

"Do you think Bruce is gay?" my brother asks.

I nod. I'm pretty sure.

"Have I ever told you I think you're gay, too?" he asks with a proud smile.

"Yes," I say. "Almost every day."

"Okay, good. Just wanted to make sure."

I hear the rapid-fire hiss of Bobby's exhaust pipe before

my father pulls up. The side door doesn't open, so he has to get out and open it with the screwdriver he keeps in his back pocket.

"Hurry, hurry," he says as he runs back to the driver's side.

"Sorry I'm late. Bobby conked out on Sunrise Highway. I had to get a cop to jump me. I don't think he's gonna survive this winter."

The car reeks of oil, and I breathe into my shirt.

"So how'd it go?" he asks.

We both shrug.

My father hums as he drives to the Dunkin' Donuts just off the highway. We go to Dunkin' Donuts every week after counseling.

It's empty aside from an older man in the corner eating alone. We sit at the counter. A pretty girl in a paper hat saunters over to us.

"What can I get for you?"

"Give me a jelly and a cup of coffee, Sweet'N Low if you have it."

I can't decide. It's between the glazed and the vanilla frosted with rainbow sprinkles. I let my brother go first.

"I'll have a chocolate glazed," he says. "And a coffee, too."

She looks at me.

"I will have...uh...the vanilla frosted with rainbow sprinkles...and some milk, please."

"You see?" my brother whispers to me. "What you just did was incredibly gay. That's what gay people order."

"Stop giving your brother a hard time," my father says.

My father has a comedy routine he likes to do whenever we go to Dunkin' Donuts. The pretty girl in the paper hat has already heard it half a dozen times, but he's going to do it again anyway.

"Miss," he says, waving her over. "We have a little bit of a problem."

She smiles and exhales. Plays along.

"What seems to be the problem tonight?" she says.

My father laughs. "Well, you see, I was gonna pay the bill, but then my son Stevie there said he wanted to pay. And then the little one here, he said he wanted to pay. Do you care who pays?"

She smiles. "No."

"Good, then you pay!"

Our block is dark except for the yellow puddles of light left by the streetlamps and a few garage doors strung with multi-colored Christmas bulbs. In the distance, we see police cars, the familiar blur of blue and red lights growing brighter as we approach, strobing against the front of our neighbors' houses, their faces awash in it as they stand on their lawns.

"What is this, now?" my father says. "Better not be your mother. I'm so sick of this bullshit. There's a goddamn restraining order, and if she did something, she's going to jail tonight."

Linda is on the front lawn, crying and smoking, surrounded by police. Her pig, Kevin, is tied to the porch banister, squealing. We head toward her and are stopped by a tall, aggressive cop.

"Hey, hey, who are yous?"

The other cops turn to look.

"I'm the tenant in the basement."

"Louie!" Linda cries. "Somebody kidnapped Katie! My baby! She's missing!"

"What do you mean? Katie the little girl? I just saw her!" my father says.

Two cops, a man and a woman, follow us into the basement. My father tosses his keys on the wobbly table and hides our dishes in the sink.

"You're catching me off guard here," he says. "Wasn't expecting company, or I would've cleaned up."

It smells like mildew, and the kitchen floor is wet in places from yesterday's rain seeping through the bottom of the door. There's a HAPPY BIRTHDAY sign tacked to the wall and another in the hallway.

The cops' radios crackle loudly with police codes.

"Somebody's birthday?" the female cop asks.

"Yeah," my father says. "Jesus's."

The cop looks at him.

Instead of celebrating Christmas, my father celebrates Jesus's birthday.

"We even have some birthday cake left over," he says and opens the refrigerator door. He pulls out a small cake with white icing and HAPPY BIRTHDAY JESUS written in broken frosting, the SUS hanging off the side.

"Thank you, but no," the cop says. "So you said you saw the little girl?"

"Yeah," he says. "You know, she's always around, usually comes grocery shopping with us."

"And when was the last time she went grocery shopping with you?"

"Stevie, when the hell was it? I never know what fuckin' day it is. What day is it?"

"Monday," I say.

"She probably came with us on Saturday morning."

"Either of you see her since?"

"I did," I say.

I look at my father to make sure it's okay to continue. "I saw her yesterday on Udall Road. She was by herself, like she always is, and we walked together for a minute."

"Did she say anything to you about where she might be going?"

"No," I say.

"Were you close?" the male cop asks me.

I shrug. "She was just my friend, that's all. Not my girlfriend. Just my friend."

The cops ask about the living conditions upstairs, Katie's relationship with Linda, with Sal; they ask about the pig, the clutter, the shit on the walls.

"Look," my father says. "I don't know anything about what they do. I just rent the basement and stay to myself. I don't even know what the relationship is between Linda and the little girl. What is she? Her aunt? Godmother? I stay out of it."

"Sometimes there's yelling late at night," my brother says.

"There's yelling?" the female cop asks.

I nod in agreement.

"Anything else?"

"No," my father says. "If we think of anything, we'll call."

The dementia unit of the nursing home smells like cafeteria food and diapers. I sit in the back of the community room and watch my father plug in his microphone and karaoke machine while Haitian nurses wheel in elderly, slack-jawed patients. My father was a singer as a younger man; he sang with bands, on the radio in a Kansas army barracks during World War II, then later, in nightclubs and bars, and later still, for fun around the house. He's older than some of the audience he sings for. He does it for the money and for the chance to get out of the house and tell a few jokes, even if the audience doesn't know he's standing in front of them. He is dressed nicely, in a blue button-down shirt and black slacks. His hair is slicked back.

He walks over to me with a stack of song sheets. "Kiddo, can you hand these out for me?"

I walk around and give one to each audience member. Some patients can't close their fingers to grasp the paper so I lay the sheets on their laps. The Haitian nurses are serving birthday cake. My brother comes in and sits next to me.

My father taps the microphone.

"Can you all hear me?"

He has a deep, pleasant voice.

"Now, we're gonna sing about eighty songs. If you have any requests, keep them to yourself. I know what I'm doing..."

He smiles. The karaoke music starts. Al Jolson. "Carolina in the Morning."

He's shuffling through the wheelchairs, crooning, smiling. Nurses in white coats hurry past the double doors. A nurse is clapping along with the beat.

"Nothing could be finer than to be in Carolina in the..."

He holds the microphone in front of an old woman so she can sing the last line.

"Are you my Jodie?!" she screams in sheer terror into the microphone.

He ignores her, keeps singing.

It's time for the comedy interlude. My father calls me up to stand beside him.

"This is my son Kenny."

I stand beside my father. He hands me a microphone.

"Kenny looks more like me, and Stevie looks more like his mother."

Vacant eyes in the audience. A man in the back is being wheeled away. My father starts the routine.

"Ya know, kiddo, I went on a date the other day."

"You did?" I say into the microphone. I'm nervous.

"Yeah, first date in a long time."

I look up at him. He puts his hand over the microphone and kneels down, prompts me with the line, "Where did you take her?" he whispers.

"Where did you take her?" I ask, my high-pitched voice echoing through the room.

"I didn't know where to take her, so I took her fishing."

"Fishing!" I say. "Did you catch anything?"

He gives the audience a deadpan look.

"God, I hope not."

On the TV, the local news is replaying interviews with police officials about Katie's kidnapping. We see a shot of Linda crying.

"Hey, hey, I know her, that woman on the TV," my father says into the microphone. "I rent the basement from her. Sad story. Little girl, cute little thing, goes to the arcade with a family friend, gets kidnapped, and they haven't seen her for four friggin' days. Can you believe that? What kind of world do we live in? Who would go and kidnap a little girl? Eight or nine. My kid's age. How old are you?"

"Seven," I say. "But she's older than me."

"Seven, eight years old and she might be dead somewhere."

The dementia patients stare at him.

I stare at him, too.

"Anyway, you all know this next song. It's called 'When You're Smiling.' If you know the words, sing along..."

The karaoke track starts.

It's a weekday evening, and I'm watching *Entertainment Tonight* on the small TV in the kitchen. Katie's been missing for seven days.

My father's cooking. "Can you get your brother up? It's almost seven and he's still sleeping. I swear if he's not your mother."

"Steve!" I yell.

My father puts a plate of fried chicken fingers in front of me. He's on his way out to see his lawyer.

"I gotta get dressed. You sure you're okay staying upstairs with Sal and Linda for a few hours?"

I nod.

"Okay, I know you don't like the pig, but maybe it'll be asleep. I don't know. Ask Linda for one of those wrestling tapes you like."

It's just after nine. My brother and I sit together on a two-seater couch in a back room cluttered with boxes and old channel-knob TVs and newspapers and milk containers and clothing and bags of cat food. We're watching *Rocky IV* through static, in the dark.

From the other room, Linda calls for Sal.

"When did Daddy say he'd be back?" I ask.

"I don't know. Hopefully soon. It smells like wet garbage in here," he says.

I giggle.

"It smells like a wet dog who's been left in a hot car."

I giggle again. He giggles when I giggle, and he tries to think of something funnier to keep me laughing.

The movie comes back from a commercial break. Apollo Creed is dancing to "Living in America."

"Do you think Katie's dead?" I ask him.

He looks at me, and for the first time I can see that he is just as scared as I am. "I don't know."

"Boys!" Linda's voice from the other room.

"Go see what she wants," my brother says.

I tiptoe through the wreckage of their guest room into their living room.

"I'm in here," Linda yells. She's smoking in the kitchen. She tells me Sal has something to show us. I call for my brother.

Sal is waiting for us in the den. We walk inside and take a seat on the couch. This might be the room he sleeps in. There's an ashtray on the table. I look at my brother. He sees a pair of scissors next to the ashtray and grabs them, sits quickly, and holds them tightly in his hand, hidden behind the crook of his leg. Sal walks in with a bowl of ice cream in one hand and a videotape in the other. He puts it in the VCR and hits PLAY before sitting down.

"Now, this is something every man should see," he says.

Squiggly lines run through the screen like a tremor, and Sal gets up to fix the tracking. The picture straightens out. On the screen appears a naked woman bent over in front of two men dressed in devil costumes.

"You guys ever seen one of these?" Sal asks.

The woman is screaming, cursing, calling the man behind her the prince of darkness. "Fuck me, my prince," she yells.

"You like that evil dick?" he asks her.

Yes, she says.

I look at my brother.

"Kenny, close your eyes," he says.

I do.

"Now, c'mon," Sal says. "He's old enough. Every man needs to see it sometime."

It's almost more graphic with my eyes closed, the moaning, the grunting, the cursing.

Sal leans closer to us and speaks slowly. He smells like booze and breath and cigarettes.

I open my eyes.

My brother grips the scissors tighter.

"Now, you see how he's fucking her there? You see what he's doing? Ken, take a look."

Sal puts his hand on my brother's shoulder.

"You see how he knows exactly how to fuck her to make her scream like that."

I look at Sal, grinding my teeth together. His eyes sag, and the crow's-feet around them crack and spread when he smiles at us.

"That's what a real man looks like," he says. "You ever seen a real man like that before, Ken?"

"Kenny, don't say anything," my brother says.

My brother clutches the scissors until they dent his palm.

Sal smiles. "The kid's gotta learn sometime."

"I think we should go," my brother says.

"You don't have to," Sal tells him.

"Yes," my brother says. "Our father will be home soon."

Linda's voice from the hall. "Sal!"

Sal takes his hand off my brother's shoulder, rises, and turns off the tape.

"Sal!" she calls again.

"What?!"

"I need my insulin shot."

He leaves the room.

The two of us sit there. My hands are shaking, and my brother is staring straight ahead with no expression.

It is our visitation weekend with my mother, and when my brother and I arrive at our nana's house, the blinds are drawn. Inside, the sharp smell of dog piss emanates from everywhere, urine-soaked carpets as hard as concrete, dog hair on the couches, sofas, on the tables, in the food, and piles of fresh dog shit hiding behind chairs and under tables. There's a family photo hung in the hallway. I stop to look as my mother leads us through the kitchen and into the living room.

"Mother! The boys are here," she yells upstairs at my nana.

"What, dear?"

"She fakes this deaf shit," my mother says. "I know it. She wants us to think she's deaf but she hears whatever the fuck she wants." She yells again. "I said, *The boys are here!*" And then she makes a gun with her fingers and mimics blowing her brains out.

Wozels yelps and starts to bark.

"Get away from Winnie!" my mother yells at her.

Winnie is my nana's dog, a small, flea-bitten Lhasa apso, sixteen years old, with one tooth left and bald from his ass down through his entire left leg. Wozels tries to play with him, and he snaps at her and growls, and Wozels jumps back, runs to me.

Winnie limps to me grumpily, and I reach out and cautiously pet his head.

"Don't put your face in his!" my mother says. "I don't feel like going to the emergency room tonight. Your father would have a fuckin' field day with that in court."

She's getting herself riled up.

"He'd say, 'Ya see, I told ya, she's a drunk, and she can't even keep the kid from getting bit by a fuckin' dog.'"

"Hello!" My nana, her hair freshly permed, comes down the steps in stocking feet, wearing a long floral dress covered with dog hair.

"Oh, look at my handsome grandsons!" she says. "And hello, little Wozels. Yes, you are so precious. Don't get jealous," she coos and laughs.

My mother brings our dinner plates out to where my brother and I sit at the table next to a small TV playing static.

"Kenneth, I forgot the wineglasses. Can you grab them out of the cupboard over the stove?"

I go into the kitchen, where the cabinets have combination locks on them.

"Nana? My mom wants some wineglasses."

"Oh, yes, dear."

She tells me she has to get her notebook, where she has the combinations written down. She'll be right back.

"You get 'em?" my mother asks.

"Nana has to get the combination for the locks," I say.

"Oh, for God's sake. She is such a nut bag. My father put her in the loony bin in 1978, and he shoulda left her there. *Mother!* No one's stealing your dishes."

Nana comes back into the kitchen with a small notebook.

"Sorry I'm such a poke," she says and giggles.

"Why do you have locks on your cabinets?" I ask her.

She gives me a serious look, cups her hand over her mouth, and whispers. "I don't want to say why in the house." And then, even lower, "They're listening."

We eat in silence except for the background TV noise.

"Oh, Winnie, get away!" Nana says. "You can't have any pot roast because you're an old man and you have no teeth."

She laughs. "He's an old grump, but I love him so," she says. "I've had him since he was just a small pup, you know. Did I ever tell you the story of how I got him?"

"Yes, twenty-five fuckin' times," my mother says. "So, Mother, tomorrow we'll go to Finast and get you some milk and eggs."

"I'm not going there anymore. I can't stand even going in that place." She looks at my brother and me and continues, "I've been going there for my groceries for fifteen years, and then they went and hired a black."

"Who?" my mother asks. "That girl who helped you to your car the other day?"

"You should've seen the way she was looking at my license plate. I'm sorry, I don't trust them."

"I know. Everyone's out to get you. You got the Mafia bugging your phones and blacks stealing your groceries."

There's breaking news on the TV. A grainy news feed of Katie, her face pale and dirty, shrouded by a blue hoodie. She's surrounded by police officers as she's rushed through mobs of media and camera flashes. She's alive. The bottom of the screen says KATIE BEERS FOUND!

"Turn it up!" my brother says.

The phone rings.

"That's probably your father," my mother says. I run to pick it up.

The news anchors recap the story: she was last seen with a family friend, John Esposito, at an arcade. Esposito, a friend of Linda and Sal's, called the police and reported her missing. There's old news footage of police searching Esposito's house, which cuts into an image of the dungeon where she was being held. The newscaster says Esposito led police into a converted garage. Behind a bookcase they found a layer of carpet and linoleum and underneath it a two-hundred-pound slab of concrete leading to a seven-foot shaft, then another tunnel leading to a six-by-seven dungeon where Katie spent seventeen days with a chain around her neck, lying in her own waste, a flickering television set in the corner her only light.

"Jesus fucking Christ, and your father knows these people? He lets you live with these pedophile motherfuckers? Kenneth, give me the goddamn phone..."

She grabs it from my hands.

"Yeah, listen, old man, you and Sal and Johnny boy are all goin' to prison, you hear me? I'm not letting my kids anywhere near you or these sick motherfuckers..."

She tells my father she's not letting us come home, that he can call the police if he wants.

She slams down the phone, then picks it back up and calls our counselor, Bruce, then her lawyer, and tells them she won't let us go back to Linda and Sal's house. There's a loud, thumping bang on the door, and we see a flicker of police lights through the drawn blinds.

My grandmother opens the door. My mother's still crying on the phone, calling my father a pedophile, a faggot, a molester. She hands me the phone, tells me to tell her lawyer I'm afraid.

"Hello?"

"Hi, is this Ken?"

"Yes," I say.

"How do you feel about living with these people you see on the news?"

"I don't know. It's scary," I say.

"Would you rather stay with your mom?" he asks.

"Yes," I say.

The police try to calm my mother. They ask her if she's had anything to drink tonight. She tells them to go fuck themselves. The lawyer wants to talk to my brother. I walk to the kitchen window. I can hear the tailpipe rumble of my father's car, then I see headlights.

"Daddy's here," I say.

"Get that motherfucker away!" my mother says. "I have a restraining order, and if he comes within a hundred feet he's going to jail."

As my father approaches the house, a police officer walks out to meet him.

"Sir, your wife tells us there's a restraining order against you."

"I want my kids."

He's got the custody papers in his hands. She comes out onto the lawn with the restraining order in her hands.

"Arrest him."

"She's not allowed to keep my kids from me. I have custody. She's a goddamn drunk."

The police yell at my father to go sit in his car, yell at my mother to stay inside.

One cop follows my mother, the other my father. More

cops have pulled up alongside the house. The neighbors are now out on their porches.

I run out onto the front lawn and ask the cop if I can sit with my father. He says yes, and I run to the car and open the door and hop inside.

"Hey, kiddo!" he says, faking a smile. "Your mother's a real bitch, ya know that? You're my kids. I have custody. She's calling me a pedophile? I don't know anything about what happened to Katie. I don't know anything about Sal. Did he touch you?"

I tell him he didn't.

"I stay to myself. Linda's a nice lady. Sal helps me get my car going in the morning. Are you scared living there?"

I'm quiet. The back door opens, and my brother climbs into the backseat.

"What's your mother saying?" my father asks.

"She wants us to stay because of what happened to Katie."

"You're not staying."

My brother tells him we're scared to live there. He tells him about the porn, about Sal's breath and his smile.

"It's just a cheap apartment I found," my father says. He looks at me and asks me if I want to stay with my mother, and I nod quietly.

"I have custody," he says. "I'll let you stay for now, a week, until all this bullshit blows over, but then you're coming home."

A cop knocks on the driver's side window, and my father rolls it down.

"We have to take you to jail," the cop says.

"You're gonna arrest me in front of my kids?"

"We have to," the cop tells him. "She has the restraining order. There's nothing we can do."

My father gets out of the car. The cop has him turn and press his chest against the window. They cuff his hands behind his back and walk him to a cop car.

"Bye-bye, Louie!" my mother shrieks. "Say hi to John Esposito for me, you child molester piece of shit."

Nana's basement is cold and unfinished, a large, dark space with no windows and exposed electrical wiring. There's a single lamp that does little to light the room and a small channel-knob TV with a rabbit-ear antenna propped up on a bar stool. A ceramic Christmas tree rests in the corner.

My brother and I sit on the concrete floor playing a game with old baseball cards. My mother is drunk in her chair, her sock-clad feet resting on a moving box she's using as an ottoman. She's watching Bob Ross paint Christmas Eve mountains. She's pissed.

"Oh, look at this asshole," she says. The ice cubes clink in her glass. "They let him on TV? With that Jew 'fro?"

The TV is half static. Bob Ross speaks in a calming lull. He's painting more trees still. Green pines. He says, "We don't make mistakes, we have happy accidents," and my mother is incredulous. Mocks his voice. "Ooh, aren't I special, every-body? I'm Bob Ross, and I have happy accidents! Please don't tell my wife I'm a fag!"

She takes a sip.

"Oh, he needs to be killed!"

My uncle's briefcase is on top of the TV. My brother thinks it'll be funny to hide it from him.

"Knock it off, Stephen," she says. "Would you want some-body hiding your stuff?"

"Do you really think that newspaper he has is worth mil-lions?" my brother asks her.

"I don't know," she says. "He says he's talking to a friend in Arizona who knows a Hollywood producer who wants to pay him a lot for it."

"Can you imagine a million dollars?" my brother asks me.

I smile. No, I say. My mother says she'd buy a house on the beach. She loves the water and tells us she wants to be reincarnated as a dolphin so she can spend her whole life swimming through clear, endless water, free and happy.

After the TV is off and my mother is asleep, my brother and I sit up and talk. The basement is so dark I can't see my hand in front of my face. Something is dripping. I think there are rats and squirrels in the walls. I move closer to my brother.

"Will you move over? You have to sit so close?"

"Are those really rats?" I ask him.

"Probably. There's bats down here, too."

"Shut up!"

"Serious. And bats can smell young blood. I'm old enough now so I'm safe, but you aren't."

I tell him he's lying just to scare me, but he insists.

Minutes pass in silence.

"Are there really bats?" I ask him.

"Yes. Now shut up."

I hear scratching from inside the walls. I'm too scared to move. My imagination takes over. I feel something crawling up my legs, but nothing is there.

"Do you hate me?" I ask him.

"No," he answers quickly, sounding hurt. "Why would you even ask me that?"

"Okay," I say. "Sometimes it seems like you do."

"That's stupid. Don't I let you hang out with my friends?" he asks.

"I know."

"And some of them make fun of you, and I always defend you, right?"

I nod. He can't see me, but it's understood.

"And I let you watch me beat Street Fighter II, right?"

"I know. That was awesome," I say and smile, remembering that night at the arcade.

"Would I do that if I hated you?"

"I guess not."

"Okay, I'm gonna tell you something, but you can't go talking about it. Not even to Wozels. Okay?"

I nod.

"The other day I heard Mommy and Uncle Carter talking. They were talking about disappearing with us to Arizona."

"They said disappear?"

"Yeah. Those exact words. Like we're gonna move and start school and hide out or something."

"What about Daddy?"

"I don't know," he says. "You can't say anything to him, though. Mommy will lose her shit."

I sit quietly, trying to picture a new life in a new place.

"What's Arizona like?" I ask.

"I don't know," he says. "Mommy says it's really nice, with palm trees and mountains. I know it's really hot. Like the hottest place on earth."

"Maybe when Uncle Carter sells his briefcase we can all get a new house," I say.

"Maybe," my brother says.

"What's so special about Uncle Carter's newspaper?" I ask him.

"It's because it's the original newspaper that documented the *Amityville Horror* murders," he tells me.

"What's that?"

"You're too young to know."

"No, I'm not."

"Okay," he begins. "It's about this guy Mommy and Uncle Carter used to know. I think his name was Tommy DeFeo. Or DeLeo. Or Ronnie. Can't remember. And one night he ran into a bar covered in blood."

"Why?"

"You gonna let me tell it?"

He goes on. "Turns out he took a shotgun and murdered his entire family. Killed them all. Everyone in his family. Dead. Can you imagine that?"

"No." And then I ask quietly, "Why?"

"Nobody knows. He ran into the bar screaming for help, but he admitted later that he killed his whole family. And he's still out there, on the loose."

"Stop it; you're just saying that."

"I mean he might be. Who knows where he is?"

"They lived around here?"

"Right around the corn—stop moving closer to me… God…seriously…he probably won't come after you. Probably."

"And the original newspaper is worth tons of money?"

My brother is quiet for a moment.

"That's what he says."

chapter 4

We're on a dark road inside a maze of barren trees heading north. Headlights burst through blackness. Tires crunch over dirty slush. My mother's driving while my uncle Carter alternates between guiding us on the map that's splayed out across his lap and drumming on the dashboard along to the Billy Joel cassette he's playing. We haven't seen a sign for what seems like an hour, maybe longer. I sit with my brother and Wozels in the back. The car floor is littered with fast-food bags, fruit chew wrappers, empty cigarette packages.

This was supposed to be one of my mother's visitation dates, but instead of driving us home, she's decided to take us upstate. She says my father's family once owned some property up here, and he once told her he hid money inside the small house, which sat on several acres of neglected forestland. When we arrive, the house is semidemolished and surrounded by knee-high grass and weeds. A few hundred feet away, there's an empty cement swimming pool. We step carefully through the grass. My mother tells us to beware of snakes.

There's a barn covered with red, chipping paint in the faraway distance.

Inside the house, wooden floorboards creak as we make our way through the rooms. We can't tell if it's been vandalized or battered by storms or both. My brother tells me black bears live in the woods, and my mother says, "Stop scaring your brother."

My uncle checks the cabinets and drawers for anything that looks like an envelope or shoe box full of money. I walk behind my mother as she goes through the kitchen cabinets, where old cereal boxes stand next to dusty teacups.

"This place should be condemned," she says. "There's nothing here anymore. Your father probably grabbed it already."

She opens the utensil drawers, which pull out crookedly, then jams them back shut, rubs her temples, and says, "That's just peachy; we drive three hours out of our way for nothing."

Night falls quickly up this way, and we pull off the gravelly road away from the property and head slowly down a dark side street, where a small sign with an arrow drawn on it points us to a motor lodge, a one-story strip of rooms in need of new paint, with a restaurant attached. A sign says NO PETS ALLOWED. My mother tells us to hide the dog, make sure she doesn't bark. She heads inside while we wait. My mother comes out with a smile and a room key. Opens the car door and tells us they have a bar inside the lobby.

The bar is Bavarian, with thick, smoky air. The woman behind the counter has a pretty face but seems standoffish. In one corner, an obese man wearing a Pantera shirt is laughing with a woman covered in tattoos. I look around the bar at all the faces scrunching and twisting as they laugh and exhale smoke. In another corner hangs a red flag bearing a black swastika. My mother and uncle sit at the bar and order two beers. I sit beside my brother.

The old man next to us has a newsboy cap pulled down over his eyes. The number 1488 is tattooed on the back of his hand. He's talking to his friend, to the bartender, to all of us.

"He was persecuted for being ahead of his time...A hundred years from now, people will look back in shame at how we treated the führer, at how we killed genius...we killed genius!"

My mother turns to us.

"You hear this fuckin' Nazi? Saying Hitler was a genius?"

My brother tells her to keep her voice down.

"Don't tell me what to do, little boy, okay?" But then she adds in a whisper, "I think we're in a fuckin' Nazi bar."

"What gave it away?" my brother says.

She seems concerned, but she tells us not to worry because her maiden name is German so we should be fine. She orders another beer. My uncle's flirting with a woman who has a tattoo on her face. I follow my brother to the pinball machine. I stand behind him and watch him play. I look over my shoulder and see two boys standing, staring at us. I look away, then back at them. Still staring. Both of them have red hair and freckles; the shorter one has a hearing aid.

I'm wearing a T-shirt that says KENNY'S DOG WOZELS under a photograph of Wozels's grinning face. My mother took my favorite photograph of Wozels to a kiosk in the mall and had it made. She gave it to me for Christmas.

"Nice shirt," says the taller one, pointing at me, laughing and cackling.

I smile shyly and nod, looking back at the pinball machine.

The shorter boy walks over to us, flicks my clip-on earring. "What's this?" he asks in an off-pitch, molasses drawl.

I am sad for him and scared of him. I can't seem to allow my eyes to meet his. I tug on my brother's shirt, and he turns around.

"What's up?"

"This your brother?"

He nods. They tell us their names: Derek and Travis. Derek, the older one, is sixteen. Travis is thirteen but looks younger, maybe around ten. I'm seven and two months, and I tell them so. Travis wasn't born deaf but won't tell us what happened. We talk about upstate New York—*Yeah, it sucks, nothing to do*—compare notes on video games, then Derek casually challenges us to a fistfight in the parking lot.

I look at my brother.

Derek repeats the challenge. He says Travis is going to fuck me up, and Travis agrees, nods, and repeats it, *Immafukooup.* I ask him why, and he tells me he's wanted to fight me since he saw me walk in wearing a clip-on earring and a T-shirt with a white fluffy dog on it. My brother nods, as if he sees their point, and signs me up to fight.

"Kenny, you can take this kid," he tells me.

I start to think of the pro wrestling I've been watching, imagine myself for a moment in face paint and flashy tights, "Welcome to the Jungle" blasting through the arena, the crowd going crazy.

"Are you sure?" I ask him.

"I wouldn't get you involved in something if I knew you'd get hurt," he says.

I nod. I trust him.

It's not even ten degrees outside. The still, windless cold burns my knuckles. My hands are shaking. Travis is punching at Derek's hands, warming up. He's fast. He's done this before. I look at my brother and wonder why he got me involved. I've never been in a fight before, and he knows that. He knows that I cry when he pours salt on slugs because I think the slugs have feelings. I don't want to fight this boy. I'm scared he'll hurt me. I'm scared I'll hurt him. I'm scared he'll rip my Wozels shirt.

My brother kneels down in front of me, puts his hand up. Asks me to throw a punch. I only know how to punch like a pro wrestler, by making exaggerated, clubbing blows while stomping my foot on the ground and making an explosion sound with my mouth.

"What was that?" my brother asks me.

"A punch?"

He stands up and tells me to put my hands up. This is how you throw a punch, he says, and he extends his arm straight out, his knuckles colliding with my palm. He does it again and again. A man comes out of the bar to smoke.

"Don't be embarrassed by your Wozels shirt," he says. "If you like it, then wear it, okay?"

I'm trying not to cry.

"You're not gonna let him talk about your Wozels shirt like that, are you?"

I shake my head.

"Let me hear you say it."

"No!" I say.

"Fuck no," he says.

"Fuck no," I repeat, sniff away my tears.

"Let me see you throw a punch," he says.

I do it as he showed me. He tells me it's perfect.

There's about ten feet between me and Travis. Our brothers are in our corners like coaches. Derek rings the imaginary bell.

We circle each other for a minute, my brother talking to me all the while, telling me to keep my hands up. I can barely make a fist. Travis is crouched down low, his fists up to his chin, while Derek yells at him. I can't make out what they're saying.

I rush Travis, charge in with a clothesline, arm extended, just like I've seen the wrestlers do. Travis charges right back at me, fearless, fury in his eyes, screaming his distorted war cry. He leaps high into the air like a ninja and jump-kicks me in the chest.

It feels as though his foot has gone right through me. The hollow thud of his running shoe against my bony chest, the dirt from his sole on Wozels's face. He knocks the wind out of me. I hit the gravel. My body twists in pain for a moment. I close my eyes, then open them wide. The sky above is black and endless, no stars, no moon, just deep black.

The fight's over.

I finally exhale and breathe in again. My brother runs up to me and makes sure Travis stays back.

Travis calls me a bitch and high-fives his brother.

My brother helps me off the ground.

"You okay?"

I shake my head.

My uncle walks out of the bar with his arm around a strange woman.

He sees I'm upset and heads toward me, looking concerned.

"What's wrong, little guy?"

I shake my head. "Nothing."

He looks over at Derek and Travis.

"Everybody getting along out here?" he asks in a big voice. I stand behind him. "Where's my mom?"

"She's in the bathroom. What happened?" he asks.

"Nothing."

"These boys picking on you guys?" he says, loud enough for them to hear.

"No," my brother says. "We were just playing around, and Kenny fell down—that's all."

Carter looks over at my brother, then at Derek and Travis.

"Why don't you two go on inside?" my uncle says, and they obey. My mother walks out, laughing, stumbling a bit, unsure which way our room is.

The strange woman asks my uncle if he's coming, waves her room key in the air.

"Nah, babe, not tonight, early day tomorrow, lots of driving, gotta get some shut-eye."

He walks me back to the room, his hand on my shoulder, and kneels down beside me.

"Those kids hurt you?"

"No," I say.

His breath is boozy, and his skin smells like smoke. I can tell he doesn't believe me. I tell him I'm okay. He nods and opens the door.

I don't sleep that night. My mother and uncle are asleep in the same bed. My brother's still awake, sitting cross-legged on the motel room carpet, watching *Real Sex 5* on mute. I lie in bed next to Wozels and watch out of the corner of my eye, mesmerized and mortified by the size of one woman's nipples. He finally shuts off the TV. I close my eyes and pretend to be asleep. He lies next to me.

"I know you're not sleeping," he says.

I wait a moment, then in my best groggy, fake-asleep voice ask, "Whatdyasay?"

"You're the worst fake sleeper ever," he says.

I roll over, give up on the ploy.

"Are we going to miss school tomorrow?" I ask him.

"We're not going back," he says. "We're going to Arizona."

"What about Daddy?" I ask him.

"I don't know, Kenny," he says.

"What about my friends?" I ask him.

"What friends?"

"I have friends," I say.

"Who?"

It's quiet except for my uncle's throaty snore.

"I feel bad I said I was embarrassed by the Wozels shirt," I say out loud.

"Don't feel bad; she doesn't know," he says.

"But I told her," I said.

"She doesn't understand what you're saying, Kenny," he says.

I stare up at the ceiling, wonder if he's right.

"Why did you let me fight that boy?" I ask him.

There's a burst of laughter outside our room.

"I thought you were a better fighter than that," he says.

I roll over to look at him. My eyes have adjusted to the darkness, and I can see the outline of his face.

"I didn't think you'd get hurt," he says. "Did it hurt?"

"No," I tell him. "It didn't hurt."

We get an early start the next morning, 6:00 a.m. We're going to try to make it all the way to Texas. We play car games.

For breakfast we stop in Kentucky, where they add mayonnaise and lettuce and tomatoes to their egg sandwiches. It's not the same as in New York. We fill up on gas, and my brother tries on sunglasses inside the gas station store while I walk Wozels in the gravel and my uncle makes a call on a pay phone. I watch him twist inside the booth, lift his Detroit Tigers hat off his head, and wipe the sweat from his brow. He's yelling, but I can't make out what he's saying. He slams the phone down and walks quickly into the store, and my mother comes out a panicked second later, crying.

"What's wrong?" I ask her.

"Get in the fuckin' car!" she says.

"What happened?" I ask my uncle.

"Your Pop Pop died," he says and climbs into the backseat.

My mother is hysterical in the driver's seat, crying, cursing, spitting.

"What are we gonna do?" she says out loud. "We're a day away from Arizona. How are we gonna get back for the funeral?"

"There ain't gonna be a funeral," my uncle says.

"Oh, knock your shit off, learn to forgive; the man's dead," she says.

"Dolph is dead," he says.

My Pop Pop's first name was Randolph, the same as my middle name. He was a bitter man, a drunk, and my mother used to joke about his German temper. They called him Dolph for short, a joke born when he decided he wanted to bring back the Hitler mustache and walked around with one for the better part of a year. He died alone in his studio apartment.

"Why don't you get the fuck out of my car and walk to Arizona?" she says. "You wanna keep making jokes about our father?"

"The man was a fuckin' tyrant!" he screams. "He ruined my goddamn life!"

"Oh, so melodramatic," she says. "He loved you."

"The fuck he did."

"How many times did he send you to Briarcliff to get sober?"

"Don't you talk to me about that in front of my goddamn nephews," he says, exploding into red-faced anger. "And you're welcome for all the goddamn money I've dished out to get you all the way across the country."

"Because we know how hard it is selling dope outside Toomey's Tavern."

"Fuck you, you cunt."

"Lovely word to use in front of my children," she says, her voice cracking. "We just lost our father, you scumbag!" She starts crying again.

We get an early start the next morning and drive mostly in silence until we see the sign that says WELCOME TO ARIZONA.

The sun is out. It's too warm for late February. Palm trees line the streets. Everything looks different here: the streets are wider and newer. The gas stations have funny names. There are fast-food restaurants we've never heard of. My mother has calmed down. She's smiling at the sights, tells us we can go swimming in winter. We all smile. Wozels is on her hind legs looking out the window, the wind in her face.

For the first few months, we live in an Econo Lodge with an ice machine and a dirty pool. Then we clean out our car and sell it to some Mexican guy and use the money to rent a nice apartment of our own in a complex of multiple stucco buildings. Its large windows overlook an irrigation canal where

I walk Wozels and kick the rocks and daydream. My mother buys a mattress, and we set it on the floor of her bedroom beside our TV and my brother's new SEGA. In the living room, she's set up some plastic patio furniture we'll use until we can afford real furniture. My uncle stays with us for a few weeks before he finds his own studio apartment with a Murphy pull-down bed and a small kitchenette. My mother spends her days looking for work, putting in applications at gas stations, preschool cafeterias, video rental stores, anything nearby.

After school, I walk Wozels on the irrigation canal while the late afternoon turns gradually to dusk. My small reflection wobbles in the black canal water and shatters to pieces when I drop a heavy stone that plunks quickly to the bottom. And then I watch myself slowly come back together as the water recollects its stillness. I feel a tug on the leash. Wozels has found a dead bird covered with ants, swarming, relentless as they each take a piece. I pull her away, and she goes back to sniffing the dusty road.

The sun is weakening, and the scent of irrigation pollutes the air. The kids are different here. They think I speak funny and make me say words in my New York accent—*coffee* and *water* and *dog*—then say *Do it again* and laugh. I can't tell if they're making fun of me or not, but I say the words in my normal voice, and they try to mimic it back. They dress different here, too, and have cool names and they've all been best friends since kindergarten and they skateboard home together and live in new houses with pink stucco roofs and trees painted white to deflect the sun.

I lead Wozels away from the canal and through the parking

lot, where she peeks under every parked car looking for cats. She makes me smile.

When I get home, dinner's on the stove, and my mother is sitting in front of our new word processor, the one she bought with her first paycheck. She got a job at a gas station up the road. She had my brother help her with her résumé and spent the last few weeks applying all over town. She works nights and takes an English class during the day at the local community college. Now she has her first homework assignment.

"Kenneth, I don't know where your brother disappeared to. Do you know anything about commas?"

I think so, I say.

"Will you read this for me and tell me if it makes sense?" she asks, then makes me promise not to laugh before she reads it out loud. It's an essay about her sister.

"My sister-comma-Gina-comma-was a very special person to me-comma-and when we were kids-comma-my father took us out east-comma-to the beach."

I walk over to her and read the big yellow letters on the black screen.

"I don't think you need this comma," I tell her. "Or this one or this one."

She hits the backspace button, erases the commas.

"Ya know, this teacher of mine's a real piece a work, a real know-it-all bitch, ya know, one of those skinny, prissy women with a face you just wanna mush...she wouldn't stop talking about the goddamn commas, comma this and comma that, don't forget the commas."

"What's the assignment?" I ask and lie on the floor with Wozels, who jumps on me and licks my face, my lips, my eyelids, licks and licks the more I laugh.

"It's supposed to be a childhood memory, and I..." she says, then pauses and looks over at me. "All right, Kenneth, enough having sex with the dog, okay? Jesus Christ, you let her lick your face like that? She was just licking her pussy!"

I stand up and wipe my face with the bottom of my T-shirt. She checks the time. It's almost seven. She's working the graveyard shift tonight. My brother comes out of his bedroom.

"I just finished *The Firm*," he says, proud.

"You boys wanna eat? I have to get going soon."

We sit together at our new dining room table. Wozels taps my leg with her paw, asks me for some macaroni by tilting her head, but I tell her no. My mother tells us another story about how much she hates her teacher, and soon we're done and she's scurrying around our living room in her uniform: men's slacks and a bulky man's shirt with a gas station logo.

I worry about her walking along the dark canal at night, but she tells me it'll be okay.

She comes home around six, makes breakfast, and wakes us up for school. It's the first night I can remember her not drinking.

In the morning, she drives me to school before she heads off to work.

"Did you finish your English homework?" she asks during our drive.

"Oh, shit!"

"What did you just say? You better never let me hear you say that again!"

I'd forgotten all about it, but I unzip my backpack and pull out my notebook and a pen and start writing.

My mother pulls the car over and watches. The assignment

is to write a story about Saint Patrick's Day, and I write about Wozels meeting a leprechaun and the two of them stealing a pot of gold and going on the run together, two bandits.

I catch her staring at me and say, "What?" and she says, "Nothing," then she asks me, "You like writing?"

I nod.

And then I lift my head up from the notebook. "Done!"

"You're done with the whole story?" she asks me.

I hand it over to her, and she reads it.

"Your teachers know you can write?" she asks me.

I shrug.

"Don't be shy," she says. "I was a very shy little girl. I was always too scared to speak up."

I can hear the warning bell, so I grab my story from my mother's hands, lean into the backseat to kiss Wozels, kiss my mother, and run to class.

It's a long day at school, and I watch the hands on the oversize clock tick by. I look up at the green chalkboard, still dirty with faded chalk from yesterday's lesson. Above it in fresh white chalk is today's date, my father's seventy-first birthday.

I walk home alone up the road and around the corner and down the canal, daydreaming and peering into the strangers' backyards. When I arrive home, my mother's on the phone with her sister.

"Okay, Ken just got home, so I'm gonna..."

"Yeah, no, Kerry, I know it's sad, but..."

She lowers the phone and makes a gun with her fingers and pretends to shoot herself in the head.

"Okay, Kenny just got home, so I have to go..."

"Okay, love you, too, bye."

She hangs up.

"Hey, kid. How was school?"

"Good," I say.

"Did your teachers love your leprechaun essay? I was just bragging to Kerry how you can write up a storm."

I shrug. "I think so."

"They're just jealous. They're probably unhappy at home."

She makes me a bologna sandwich as I sit in front of a *Saved by the Bell* rerun and try to think of a way to bring up my father's birthday.

"Your father turns seventy-one today," she says casually, before I can, and sets the plate down in front of me. "Is he a hundred yet? Old prick. Do you know he lived at home until he was fifty years old? Even his mother thought he was a homo."

"Do you think we should call him?"

"No. You're not calling the old prick; he has caller ID, and he'll find out where we are and he'll come out here with his lawyer buddy, that fat, bald motherfucker."

Zack is in trouble with Mr. Belding again. The laugh track erupts.

She's shuffling in the kitchen.

"You know how to block a number?" she asks me.

"No," I say.

"I think it's star eighty-two," she says, picking up the phone. "Go ahead and call him, just block the number."

I nod okay. I have his number memorized: 242-9734.

I mute the TV and start to dial. She waits for me to finish, then picks up the other phone to listen to our conversation.

"If he asks, you don't know where we are!" she says through clenched teeth. "You know nothing, understand?!"

I nod.

The phone rings.

My father's voice is on the line. "Hello?"

"Daddy?"

"Who's this? Stevie?"

"It's Kenny!"

He sounds relieved, excited, worried.

"Baby, where are you?"

My mother is whispering angrily into the phone. *"You don't know shit, you are nowhere, tell him you don't know!"* not realizing that my father can hear her.

"Uh...I don't know where I am," I say.

He sighs.

"Are you safe?"

Yes, I say.

"Is your mother listening on the other end?"

"No, I'm not!" she yells, incredulous. "Now go die, ya old fuck!"

It's quiet for a moment.

"Happy birthday!" I say, and he says thank you and tells me he went out for coffee and crumb cake at a diner with a new friend he made, some man named Tony, whom he met in the basement of church at a support meeting for fathers who've lost their children.

"Oh, give me a fuckin' break," my mother whispers into the other end. "How pathetic! Probably jerked each other off, too."

"Are you gonna keep interrupting?" he yells.

"Anyway," he says. "How are you?"

"I'm good. I'm getting ready for Field Day. Lots of running with my PE class."

"They call it PE? New Yorkers call it gym class."

"Yeah, it's different here," I say.

"Where?"

"You shut the fuck up, you don't know, you tell him you don't know, goddamn it!" my mother whispers violently, her finger over her mouth.

"My school has a band," I say, "and I think I'm going to join it instead of chorus."

My father plays the clarinet, and when I tell him I want to play the trombone he is a little sad, asks me if I considered the clarinet. "It's lighter, and they get more solos, and I could teach you some of the basics..."

"Die, die, die, die, die..."

My mother's voice is barely audible.

"Die, die, die..."

He pauses, loses his train of thought, and starts again.

"I could even send you my old clarinet."

It's quiet again.

"Is Stevie around?" he asks.

"I'm not sure where he is."

"Okay, well, thank you for calling, kiddo."

"Sure. Happy birthday again."

"Maybe sometime you can come visit me?" he asks, his voice cracking.

I hate it when he cries. It makes me sad, and I'm not very good at keeping myself from crying.

"You know, I'm their father—you can't keep them from me!" he screams at my mother.

"Okay, time to get off the phone!" my mother yells, barreling toward me. She grabs the phone and tells him to go fuck little boys and slams the phone down.

I unmute the TV.

chapter 5

My uncle Carter bows to me in his karate *gi*, a lit cigarette in his hand, and takes his stance about five or six feet away from me in our kitchen. He tells me to put my hands up. "This is called a backhanded spin punch."

I'm pretty sure he makes the names up.

He spins and lunges at me, barely misses my palm with the glowing orange tip of his cigarette.

"When I sell my newspaper and get my hands on the green, I'm gonna buy you some karate lessons," he says. "You have to learn to be a man. This is a roundhouse spin kick..."

He spins and extends a long leg at me, his foot barely missing my face. I hate when he practices.

"And I think you should start going by Ken. Ken's a man's name. Ken fucks your girlfriend. You don't wanna be known as Kenny. Kenny's a skinny black guy with a squeaky voice. You don't want to grow up as Kenny. They call this an open-palm spin chop..."

He spins and chops at my face, barely misses.

He's hopping on one foot because that's what they do in the movies.

"Carter, we have neighbors. Stop your fuckin' hopping!" my mother yells from the living room.

He mumbles under his breath, "Little guy, can you grab me a brewski?" I open the refrigerator and grab a can of beer. Toss it to him, and he opens it with one hand and takes a swig, the foam settling in his mustache.

"Now I'm gonna combine a jumping scissors kick with a backhanded open-palm jab. Ready?"

I give him an uncertain nod.

He leaps up into the air and scissors his legs, kicks at my face, barely misses, spins, and backhand-chops me in the face, his cigarette jamming into my mouth.

I fall backwards into a bag of dog food and spit out the ash from the cigarette.

"You okay, little man?" He looks sincerely concerned.

I tell him I am, but the ash taste lingers in my mouth.

"I'm so sorry. Oh, man, I'm so sorry. What happened?"

He takes a step backwards, slips, and falls with a crash into our opened dishwasher, smashing into the plates, mugs, glasses, silverware. The dishwasher bends but doesn't break, and he lets out a gasp with his head still up, then his neck hangs and he lies still.

Oh, shit, I think.

His lanky frame is splayed out on top of the dishwasher, his arms and legs motionless, his mouth wide open, eyes closed. I can't tell if his chest is moving.

I go into the living room, where my mother's watching *Home Improvement*.

"What is it?" she asks.

"I think Uncle Carter's dead," I say.

"What?" She races into the kitchen. "Are you kidding me? Carter!"

She rushes toward him, avoiding the shards of glass, the blood, the small splinters of broken plates.

"Carter?" And then louder: "Carter?" She studies him for a moment. "He's fine. He's faking it."

My brother comes out of his bedroom.

"What's going on?"

"Come here and help me get your uncle out of the dishwasher."

"He's not dead?" I ask her.

"No. He's just an asshole."

I grab one of his legs. My brother grabs an arm. My mother grabs the other arm.

"What did I tell you about doing karate in the goddamn kitchen? Look at this shit, broken plates and dishes. I just bought this shit. You know I'm not made of money."

Wozels walks into the kitchen, sniffs the glass, the beer, the blood.

No, I say and shoo her away. I tell her to stay out of the kitchen. I tell her I don't want her cutting her paws. She sniffs the air.

"Okay...Carter?!...you can stop faking it now."

He lifts his head up, groggy, half drunk, his chin tucked into his neck.

We all help pick him up. He's heavy. Dead weight.

We all stand around him while his eyes adjust. And then he starts laughing. And my mother shakes her head and laughs, then we laugh, too.

"All right, everybody out of the kitchen so I can sweep up

this glass. Just what I need before I go to work. More cleaning! Boys, help him into your room."

My brother and I put his arms over our shoulders, and I struggle as we walk him to our bedroom. My mother starts the vacuum. Wozels hates the vacuum, and she barks and hides under the table.

My brother and I sit him down on the bed, and my mother comes in with some Band-Aids and Listerine.

"What's the Listerine for?" Carter asks her.

"I don't have any disinfectant."

"You're not putting fuckin' Listerine on my gash."

"It's the same shit," she says.

He starts laughing again. His laugh is infectious, and we all start laughing as my mother pours Listerine on his cuts and cleans him up.

"You're such an asshole," she says to Carter and kisses him on the head. "He's been like this since he was eight years old," she tells my brother.

My uncle starts doing his impression of Dana Carvey's impression of George H. W. Bush, and they laugh.

"What a clown," she says.

Carter's in a silly mood now—we all are—and he asks me to bring him the phone and a phone book.

He sits up in the bed and pages through the thick book until he finds the number for the pharmacy up the road.

A woman answers. Carter tries to mimic an old woman's voice: "Hello, yes, I called earlier. Have you gotten my hemorrhoid cream yet?"

I giggle with my hand over my mouth, looking over at my brother to make sure he's giggling, too.

"Yes, the hemorrhoid cream for my ass."

Kenny Porpora

"No, it burns and I need my cream, you bastard!"

And then he hangs up. Laughs. Flips through the pages. Calls Pizza Hut. Now he's effeminate, using a husky, lisping voice: "Yes, I called about the pepperoni…"

"No, I don't want a pizza, I just want the pepperoni…"

"Yes, and extra sausage."

"Yes, no, it's actually for my ass…"

We laugh too loudly, blowing his cover, and he hangs up.

My brother wants a turn.

"You better be blocking these calls," my mother says and smiles, shaking her head. "I don't need cops at my door."

My brother wants to call the video store up the road. He tries to do a Middle Eastern accent, but it comes out sounding Jamaican.

"Yes, I'd like to rent a movie…"

"I'd like to rent *Jugs Part Two*…"

I laugh and look at my uncle.

"Yes, I love big jugs…"

He laughs and hangs up in a hurry.

I want a turn.

My mother says I'm too young. Carter tells her it will be fine.

I want to call the video store, too, like my brother.

Carter dials. I'm not very good at accents, so I impersonate my brother's Jamaican accent.

"Yes, hello, I'd like to rent the movie *Jugs Part Two*…"

The video store clerk hangs up immediately.

"You're a retard," my brother says to me.

And then the phone rings. He's calling me back. I am petrified. I look at my brother. "Did you block the number?" my mother asks.

"Uh..."

It rings again. Again. Keeps ringing. I imagine myself getting hauled off to jail for making crank calls.

I pick up the phone.

"Uh...hello?"

It's not the video store clerk. It's a different voice, a somber one. He asks if he can speak with my mother.

"Oh. May I ask who's calling?"

He tells me he's a doctor from a hospital in New York.

"Oh, okay," I say. The laughing has stopped. My family stands around me looking confused.

I hand the phone to my mother. "It's a doctor from New York. He says he needs to talk to you."

"Now what?" she says, then, "I'll pick it up outside."

She turns the corner into the living room, out of sight, and picks up the receiver.

"All right, Ken, I've got it."

I hang up. Look at my brother, at my uncle.

We don't speak, just wait in silence.

And then she screams her painful scream. I close my eyes.

She storms into our room, crying, hysterical, spitting out her words too quickly.

Her oldest sister was found dead in her house.

Carter sits up. "Kathy?"

"Kathy! What the fuck is going on?!"

"Goddamn it!" Carter yells and punches the soft wall beside him, smashes it until it caves in and the insulation bubbles out.

"Stop with the fucking punching! I'm going fucking crazy!"

"What happened?" my brother asks.

Wozels is barking.

My uncle stands up, holding his bandaged arm, and limps into the living room. Slams our bedroom door. I wait there with my brother and listen to their screams through the walls.

My mother's drinking in the dark. The TV is off. Just she and her glass, ice cubes clinking. Some light sneaks in through the window, casting shadows.

"C'mere, pretty girl," she says to Wozels, who jumps up on the couch and lies beside her.

"Do you see Kathy in heaven?" she asks Wozels. "Can you talk to Kathy?"

Wozels tilts her head and looks at her.

"I'm sorry about Aunt Kathy," I tell her.

"She loved you so much, you know?"

She reaches out and rubs and touches my face, runs her hand through my hair.

"Do you remember her holding you, back in our apartment in the Bronx, and she'd feed you cherry vanilla ice cream and you just loved it? You were so precious."

She feels around the table for her glass.

"You were probably too young to remember. But she just loved you to pieces."

Her head falls again. It's quiet.

"Uh, Mommy?"

"What is it, baby?"

"Today's Wednesday," I tell her in a small voice.

"Today's Wednesday?" she repeats back. "So what?"

"Aren't you gonna be late for class?"

She takes a sip. Chuckles.

"No," she says. "Class was canceled."

Takes another sip.

"Fuckin' bitch with her commas. She can fuck herself, too. With her turtlenecks. I'm already beyond that class. I could *teach* that fucking class. I'll go back to school when I feel like going back."

"What about your job?" I ask her.

"Kenneth, go play in your room or something. Leave me the fuck alone. I was having a very nice time out here by myself, okay? Thank you."

She rests her head back, mumbling. Pets Wozels.

"You're my friend, aren't you?" she says to Wozels. "Yeah, you love your mommy. You're my girl."

Her words turn to whispers, and soon she's asleep.

It's the weekend, and music blasts through our living room, which is filled with balloons and streamers and cases of beer. They're throwing a party for my aunt Kathy to celebrate her life. My mother's put old photographs of her, a young girl, smiling with pigtails, on the dining room table. She's made chili using Kathy's recipe and bought a half gallon of cherry vanilla ice cream and Kathy's favorite type of vodka.

She sees me looking at some of the photos.

"Isn't that far out?" she says. "I thought we lost all our photo albums in that goddamn storage unit, but I found a few. Look how young! She's probably eight years old here."

My mother tells me a story about how it was my aunt Kathy's dream to be a ballet dancer. She could never get down to the right weight, though, liked ice cream a little too much, but she'd stand on her tiptoes and watch the local dance troupes practice in empty auditoriums and imagine that she would be in one of them someday.

My uncle arrives with his new girlfriend, Sheryl, and a few friends we don't know. They carry six-packs of beer, liquor bottles. The doors open, and the music escapes. One of our neighbors is having a cigarette on the steps outside, but he tells us not to worry about the noise. He comes up for a beer.

Hours later, my family is attempting a game of charades.

My uncle holds up three fingers.

Three words.

Mimes an old-time movie camera.

It's a movie.

He looks at the card. Stumbles back. Sheryl holds him up.

He starts dancing.

"Dancing!" I shout out.

My mother guesses *Flashdance.*

He shakes his head.

Points to me and makes claws and growls.

"Dog!"

No.

We're all yelling out names.

"Fierce!"

"Tiger!"

"Dancing tiger!"

He grabs Sheryl's hand and starts dancing, then points to her.

"Dancing with..."

"*Dances with Wolves!*" my brother yells out.

Sheryl hits him in the chest in mock offense.

My mother makes a drink in the kitchen. A stranger whispers to my uncle, motions for him to join them in the bathroom. They go into the bathroom together and close the door.

Hours later, probably 10:00 p.m.

My uncle's passed out in a chair. Sheryl's slid down the bathroom wall. Her vomit wades in the toilet. She won't or can't move. There's a man asleep in my room. A few people are leaving. I'm in the kitchen with my mother, who's telling our downstairs neighbor about *The Amityville Horror.*

"Yeah, man, I was in class with Dawn DeFeo. We knew the whole family."

"That's wild," he says. "So was the house really haunted?"

"Oh, no, that's bullshit, movie stuff. But Carter—Carter, where are you?" she peeks her head around the corner and sees him unconscious in a chair. "Oh, he's bombed...but yeah, Carter has the original newspaper from the *Amityville Record,* and he's gonna sell it to some movie producers."

Our neighbor nods.

I walk into the living room in my pajamas, barefoot, looking for my dog. "Wozels, let's go to sleep."

The front door is open. I look at my mother.

"Where's Wozels?"

She looks around. "I don't know. Did she get out?"

I run out the door, barefoot, down concrete steps, through the parking lot, onto the pebbles, the warm pavement.

"Kenneth!" She yells from behind me.

I run the route we usually take, screaming for Wozels.

"Wozels!"

I run through the apartment complex in a panic. Strangers are drinking by the barbecue pits. I ask them if they've seen a little white doggy.

"Nah, man."

And I keep running.

"Wozels!"

There are more people by the dirty pool, but they haven't seen her.

Tears blur my vision. I am running in circles. I head to the back of the complex and jump a concrete wall onto the dark canal, run to the top of a hill, and stand under a bright white moon and scream for her.

"Wozels!"

I run along the canal. I can feel I've cut my foot, but I keep running. I recklessly flail down the hill and into a gutter where the irrigation water floods the fields and I look into a dark tunnel and scream into the blackness.

"Wozels!"

Nothing. Just my hollow echo.

My hands are coated with soft dirt, and it mixes with my tears when I wipe my eyes. I sit down on the dirty ground, hunched over, knees to elbows, mutter to myself, and cry for my puppy, for my father, for my aunts and my grandfather. A stranger passes by, stops, clicks off his Walkman, and asks me if I'm okay. I look up, trudge up the hill, hyperventilating.

"Have you seen a little white doggy, by chance?" I ask him.

"Ah, you lost your dog? I'm sorry, man, I haven't. But I'll keep an eye open."

I nod. Wipe my eyes.

I run back to the apartment, up the steps, and through the door that's still open.

"You find her?" my mother asks from the kitchen.

"No!" I say, and hearing the word come out of my mouth breaks my heart. "Can we drive around and look for her?"

My mother's eyes are vacant, and she holds onto the back of the couch as she slowly lowers herself onto it and sits.

"I can't fuckin' drive right now, Kenneth! We'll look for her in the morning!"

I can't speak. Just look at her. She's not really awake. I want to scream and punch the walls, but instead I just stand quietly and watch her drift away on the couch.

I run back out the door, head north on the dark canal, stepping on stubby rocks and sharp pebbles, call her name, scream it. At the end of the canal is a main road that leads to my new school. Cars race by. I imagine her running between them.

Please, God, don't let her get hit.

I cross the street and run into the residential neighborhood of quiet homes. I scream her name again. I want to knock on every door, but it's too late at night. There's a group of kids on the corner, huddling on their bikes, chatting and laughing.

It's some of the boys from my class.

Shit. I try to turn around and walk the other way without their noticing.

"Hey! New York!" one of them calls after me.

I keep my head down and wipe my face with the bottom of my shirt. I widen my eyes before I turn around.

"Hey!"

They ride up slowly on their bikes and surround me.

"You okay, man?" one of them asks. Another laughs.

"Yeah, yeah, yeah, I'm fine. Just allergies. Not used to the desert."

"You sure you ain't been cryin'?"

I laugh. Ha! No. Crying? No. Just allergies.

Okay, they say. It's quiet.

"Fuck," I say, hoping the curse might distract them, make them see I'm cool and not sobbing alone on a dark street with dirt and snot on my T-shirt.

"So who do you hang out with?" they ask me.

"Oh, my brother has a bunch of older friends, we usually hang out at their place, do New York stuff."

They laugh, tell me I'm crazy. I smile.

"I should probably be getting home."

One of them, a blond boy with a backwards hat, looks down at my feet.

"Where are your shoes, man?"

I look down. My feet are dirty and bleeding.

"Oh, yeah," I say with a laugh, shrugging. "Sometimes I like to run around the neighborhood with no shoes."

"Is that a New York thing?"

I nod.

"Okay, well, we'll see you at school, dude."

And they're off on their bikes, riding away. "Later, New York!"

I sit on the curb and exhale. Lie backwards and look up at the sky. It looks endless, black, softened with stars. I get up and look at the house behind me. It doesn't look at all like my house in New York, but it reminds me of it. And I can see my father throwing the ball with my brother, correcting his batting stance, and my mother taking pictures, setting up the sprinkler so I can run through it.

I head home down the canal, back the same way I came, through the parking lot. And then I see her, little Wozels, sitting by our car. She sees me and starts wagging her tail, looking up at the door handle, wanting to go for a ride. I catch my breath before I run up to her and hug her. Kiss her. I hold her close and cry into her soft white fur.

I look at her and allow myself to believe she came back just for me. And then I tell her we'll go for a ride tomorrow.

Yes, I say. I promise. Tomorrow.

chapter 6

Wozels is getting a bath.

She's afraid of the water, and she cowers in the back end of the tub, her tail slunk between her legs, as the water pools around her muddy paws. My mother squirts shampoo into her hand and rubs it into Wozels's white fur. I pour water over her, and she shakes it off, spraying it at us like machine-gun fire, and I shield myself as we both laugh.

"That's a good baby girl," my mother says.

She lifts Wozels from the tub and rubs her aggressively with the towel before setting her free to run through the house like a wild bull, bucking and slipping and rubbing her face against the carpet.

The phone rings, and I go to answer it.

"If it's QVC again, tell 'em to scratch my ass, please," my mother says. "They're not getting another dime from me for that bullshit juicer."

She runs into the other room to hide, as if the caller can see her, as I pick up.

"Hello?"

"Is this Steve or Kenny?" asks a female voice.

"This is Kenny. Who's this?"

"Oh, hi, sweetie, this is Sheryl, your uncle's friend. Is your mom home?"

"Sure, one sec," I say. "Mom!"

She peeks her head around the corner. "Who is it? Tell them I'm in the shower."

"It's Sheryl, Uncle Carter's friend."

She considers it, then tells me to tell her she's out. "I'm at Albertsons buying milk," she says.

"Just take it," I say and hand her the phone.

"Hello?"

"Yeah, no, I was just out at Albertsons. What's up? Everything okay?"

She nods as she listens.

"Oh, Jesus. Okay," she says. "Yeah, I'll be right over."

The three of us stand outside Sheryl's apartment on a sidewalk bleached by the sun. My mother knocks again, and the door opens a crack, then wider once Sheryl sees who it is. She thanks us for coming and leads us through the gray, shadowy hallway into the back bedroom. My uncle lies still on the bed, his hair matted with sweat, his eyes turning yellow, and I hear my mother say it's because his liver's not working like it should. Beside the bed are a few dozen small bottles of vodka, Coca-Cola bottles full of dark yellow piss, and a motel ice bucket full of cigarette butts.

My uncle found out a few days ago that the newspaper he's been carrying around with him is worthless. He went home and started drinking almost nonstop for days, drinking until he'd pass out, wake up, and start again, until Sheryl called my mother.

"Kel, you okay?" my mother asks. His birth name is Kelly, but she almost never calls him that.

He gestures to her to come closer. My mother leans in, and he asks her if she will kill him.

"He's been asking me all day," Sheryl says. "I'm sorry you have to see this."

"Yeah, actually, why don't you two go outside and let me and Sheryl talk," my mother says to me and my brother.

Carter notices me and attempts a smile.

"Hey, little guy, how's school? How'd your solar system come out?"

"Good," I say with a half smile.

"Go on outside," my mother says again.

The next week, when we arrive home from the grocery store, I grab Wozels's leash and take her to the corner to sniff the grass before I lead her up to our apartment. When I reach the top of the stairs, I see that our front door is cracked open and there's broken glass on the concrete patio.

My mother and my brother are behind me.

"What the fuck is this?" my mother says.

She tells me to watch the glass, steps around it, and pushes the door open.

Our apartment is ransacked, in ruins. Our dining room table has been turned upside down, the TV is gone, the plates she bought smashed on the kitchen tile. The couch has been shredded, its stuffing exposed like that of a butchered animal.

"Hello?!" she yells. Nobody's there.

She stands in the middle of the room. I stand beside her,

and a sense of violation comes over me. Somebody has been here, stood where we're standing.

"My baseball cards!" my brother yells. He runs into his room and checks under his bed. They're gone.

In the kitchen, my mother sees the cookie jar smashed to pieces on the floor. "All my goddamn money!" she screams. Wozels sniffs the broken plates, the clothes on the floor. Almost everything is destroyed, and what remains is not in its right place, like the aftermath of a natural disaster.

"Goddamn motherfuckin' life!" she cries into her hands. I touch her hand.

"Not right now, okay, Kenneth?!"

I step away.

"Stephen, run to the office and tell them to call the cops, please... they're probably the motherfuckers that did it... fuckin' thieves..."

In the gray-blue dusk, we sift through the wreckage, trying to keep a mental list of everything we've lost. Books, toys, photos, video games. Each new realization knocks the wind out of me. I hear the sounds of police radios, footsteps on the stairs. The cops are tall and imposing, and their presence in our living room is a heavy one. Their radios are loud. The dispatcher's distorted voice crackles through static, calls out random codes. Their belts look heavy, too. Wozels barks at the cops and hides in the kitchen. She doesn't like men in hats. My brother explains what happened to one of the police officers, who asks my mother if she has apartment insurance. She says she doesn't and starts crying.

"Mom, c'mon," my brother says, embarrassed.

My uncle bangs on the door. His hand is bandaged. He looks sober, clear-eyed, concerned.

"What happened?"

My mother sees him and starts crying again. "Carter, they took everything!"

He looks around the apartment in disbelief, then yells angrily, "Those motherfuckers!"

The cops ask him to stay calm. He hugs my mother and looks over her shoulder to ask my brother and me if we're okay. We nod and say we are.

The cops ask him who he is. He says he's her brother. Says he didn't see anything.

"What happened to your hand?" my mother asks him.

The cops look at him.

"Sliced it opening a Bud," he says.

The cops wander through our house.

"So what happened to your hand?" my mother asks him again, almost challenging him.

"I sliced it wide open on a bottle," he says.

She looks at him.

"Ma'am, any reason to believe anyone would do this? Any recent arguments, hostile co-workers?" one of the cops asks.

She shakes her head.

They ask her about any criminal activity in the area. She says no.

Any recent break-ins in the apartment complex? No.

Any drug addicts? Anyone like that who might be capable of doing this? No.

"You know what?" my uncle says. "Actually, I think I remember seeing a coupla black guys running down the canal. I didn't even think anything of it, but I definitely saw a few black kids, probably early twenties."

"Were they carrying my fuckin' TV, Detective?" my mother asks Carter.

He doesn't know.

"Then it was probably just a bunch of black guys running around."

The cops tell us they'll keep an eye open and call us if they hear anything.

My mother beeps the horn again, a long, angry honk this time.

"He's been doing this since he was thirteen years old, keeping people waiting...I told him eleven."

My uncle Carter comes out of his apartment carrying a cooler full of beer. He opens the trunk and sets the cooler down and hops in the front seat.

"Grand Canyon!" Carter exclaims.

We play our usual car games on the way up north.

"Hey, Ken, I see the color and the color is...red!" my mother says.

I search the road for red cars, red on the billboards. Red on Wozels's collar. Soon it's quiet, just the hum of the engine and the radio. My uncle's hand out the window, the smoke from his cigarette blowing back into the car. Wozels paws me for some water, and I struggle with the plastic container of water.

"Don't get it all over," my mother says.

And then the sound of Wozels's tongue lapping up water, baby splashes, makes me smile.

The sun is setting when we get there just after five. My mother's tired from driving. My uncle is being silly in the gift shop, trying on women's hats, making us laugh. We wander around the rim of the canyon. Wozels pulls me, and I tell her no. The canyon seems neverending, almost incredible to me. My brother's not impressed.

Not too far away, a tour guide explains some of the history to a group of tourists in fanny packs and oversize Arizona T-shirts and visors and Birkenstocks. He tells them about the ghosts of the canyon, the stories of those who went down and never returned, and one woman whose spirit still haunts the canyon.

My mother asks my uncle if he'll take a photograph of us. She hands him the disposable camera. He has trouble with his bandaged hand. We huddle together, and I kneel and put my smiling face next to Wozels's.

"Ready?" he says. "Grand Canyon on three!"

He clicks the button. A small flash.

My mother rubs my head. She's softly crying beneath her sunglasses.

"You okay, Mommy?" I ask her.

"Leave me alone, okay, Kenneth?" she says, and walks away, looking at the sprawling canyon in the other direction.

I look over at my uncle, and he smiles, gives me a thumbs-up with his bandaged hand, and I wonder if he thought about me when he was punching through our window, rummaging through our house, stealing everything we had. I wonder if he knew how it would break his sister's heart. I imagine him at the pawn shop, trading everything he stole for a handful of crumpled twenties, then chopping up the powder it bought on the plate and snorting away my brother's baseball cards and the seven hundred dollars my mother had saved in the teddy-bear-shaped cookie jar on our kitchen counter and the TV and the wallet my father gave me.

And then I stare out into the endless wide-open space, the simple smallness of my body beneath this sky, a perfect spiral of cloud and fire tethered to the softest shades of blue and pink I can imagine, and my own shadow beside me as I look out over the spirits, pretending I can see them, every one of them, waving as they float away and dissolving into the sweet emptiness of dusk.

chapter 7

"Kenneth?"

A woman's whisper, her soft hand on my shoulder. It's my teacher. I look around the empty classroom. The other kids are still at recess.

"Sweetie, they want you in the principal's office," she says.

"Did I..." I clear my throat. "Did I do something wrong?"

"I don't know why they want you. They just called and told me to send you up."

I step out of the dark classroom and into the blinding brightness of the midafternoon sun. I walk along the sidewalk, past the kids playing four square and tetherball and kickball, and through the heavy double doors into the quiet library, where the kids who haven't made friends yet make friends with each other and trade pogs, up the ramp and toward the principal's office, a large room enclosed in glass. I see a police officer standing nearby, then another, and I hear the crackle of a radio. I wonder for a moment if this is about that crank call, but then I remember my brother telling me I can't go to jail for that.

Inside the principal's office I see another police officer and a man with a mustache wearing a shirt and tie. The principal is a pretty woman in her midforties with gentle eyes and a short haircut, and she tells me the man with the mustache is a detective and he's going to take me to see my father, who's waiting at the courthouse.

"How did you find us?" I ask.

"We can talk all about it in the car, okay?" he says. "For now you need to go back to your classroom and pack up your book bag and meet us outside those big blue double doors. Okay, buddy?"

He's talking to me as though I'm a baby, and I don't like him or his mustache, but I obey.

As I return to the front of the school with my WWF backpack slung over my shoulder and duck into a black unmarked police car, the other kids stand on the jungle gym and monkey bars, staring at us as we drive away.

My mother and my brother are already at the courthouse. Upstairs, my father and his lawyer are waiting for us. They separate us all into small, sterile rooms, and when it's time, some woman comes in to explain to me that my father still has full custody and a court order to take us back to New York.

"What about my mother?" I ask, and the woman tells me the judge will decide.

"What about Wozels?" I ask, and I panic at the thought of not getting to see her ever again.

She doesn't answer me.

The woman leads me down a hallway, where I see my father waiting at the end of the hallway.

"Hey, kiddo!" he says, and runs over to me, kneeling down

and encircling me in a hug. He exclaims when he sees my brother, hugs him, too.

"Do you know where Mommy is?" I ask him just before my mother's voice explodes like a shotgun from a conference room down the hallway.

"Fucking guinea cocksuckers!"

The next morning I board a plane to New York with my father and my brother. We touch down on Long Island, where the trees are half barren and the leaves are already piling up on the ground, and drive home down Jericho Turnpike in silence, my father humming, and we pass the block where his apartment used to be and keep driving, making a right turn onto Udall.

"Where are we going?" I ask him.

"I wanna make a quick stop."

This is the way to our old house, the one that was foreclosed on. We make a left onto Longshore Street and drive past familiar houses, and he slows the car as he pulls up in front of the house where we used to live. The windows are still boarded up. A Century 21 sign is hammered into the front lawn.

SOLD.

The three of us walk onto the overgrown lawn, up the horseshoe driveway, and around the back, where the paint on the garage is chipped and peeling. The grass in the backyard is longer, too, parts of the ground still deadened from the snowy winter. My father walks up the back porch steps, a heavy stone in his hands. He looks around. Knocks gently with the stone on the glass half of the flimsy storm door, then again, harder this time, and finally breaks a small square of the glass with the stone.

"Get back," he says.

He picks up a brick used to prop open the door and breaks the remaining shards of glass, then he reaches through and unlocks the door.

"What are you doing?" I ask.

He opens the door, and we step together into our old house. It still smells the same, but it's empty now. Cold. I see the exposed pipes from where the sink used to be, the refrigerator. On the wall, I see faded pencil marks—4'2" 5/1/90—and I smile. I'm a little bit taller now.

"Dad, what are we doing?" my brother asks.

My father opens the basement door, and we follow him down creaky steps into the stuffy, mildewed air. The basement is empty. Two big rooms and a boiler room we used to use for storage.

He asks us if we remember a guy named Joe DiPico. We don't. Joe's an old friend of his. They used to play together as kids, walk Jamaica Avenue in Queens and buy Cokes for a nickel. They stayed in touch and met again in the basement of a church at a meeting for fathers who had lost their children. My father tells us they started having coffee and talking. He told Joe he couldn't afford to buy the house back, and Joe offered to put a down payment on the house and said he'd keep it in his own name. My father says he's going to keep earning money singing in nursing homes and will pay Joe every month so that he can live here, in the basement at first, and he says we can live here, too.

I smile.

He says we can't tell our mother, and we both nod. He looks at my brother and says it again: "I'm serious, Stevie, not a fuckin' word to her, or she'll have us all in court," and my brother nods.

My father's lawyer told him having us living with Linda and Sal could cost him custody, told him to get us out of that apartment, show the judge we're in a safer place. We'll live here in the basement of our own house.

We walk upstairs. Through the kitchen. I walk down the halls, where there are fist-size holes in the walls. My bedroom looks smaller, but the walls are still yellow and orange. The foreclosure notice is still on my window.

"Let's get out of here," my father says, and we leave together out the back door.

I register for third grade at my old elementary school and try to settle into a new life without my mother or Wozels. My mother has moved back to New York to live with Nana but still pays rent on our apartment in Arizona. She wants to keep it for us, even leaving our bedrooms the way they were when we left. She is not allowed to see us or even come within one hundred feet of us, but she continues to fight for custody.

The first few months pass slowly. I miss Wozels, walk our gray blocks alone, and pretend she's walking beside me. I've started writing more. During recess, I sit alone at cafeteria tables and write short stories in my notebooks. I ask for tons of notebooks for my birthday, the ones with college-ruled lines, and I carry them with me, pretend they're my friends, and write anything that comes to mind. Something about my stories makes me happy, allows me to drift away a bit. On parent-teacher night, my teacher, Ms. Rutigliano, tells my father she's noticed my writing. She tells him I'm pretty good and shows him one of my stories, which he puts on our refrigerator with a magnet.

It's spring of 1995, a few days before my father's seventy-fourth birthday, and he's crouched inside the tub, scrubbing the tile with a Brillo pad.

"Kiddo, what time is it?" he calls down the hall.

It's just before noon, and Child Protective Services will be here soon for their monthly checkup. My father has set roach traps, picked up the kitchen, and gotten a haircut, and now he's cleaning before they come to ask questions and take photos and scribble in their notebooks. Our report cards are thumbtacked to the walls, and newly developed photos of us smiling are pinned with magnets on the refrigerator. We've been practicing our answers.

A knock at the door.

My father runs into his room to throw on a dress shirt and slacks over his undershirt and briefs. My brother turns off the TV, and we answer the door together with a smile.

A pretty young black woman and a middle-aged white man stand at the door with clipboards, smiling, and introduce themselves to us. My father comes into the kitchen and shakes their hands, too. The man starts taking notes, looking around, in the sink, behind the refrigerator. Peers at the photos on the refrigerator and makes a note. Asks if he can walk down the hall to check out the bedroom. My father says yes.

"So how have things been going?" she asks.

We nod to indicate they're good.

"School?"

"Very good," my father says. "I like to put their report cards up for company to see. Good grades. They're good kids."

The woman asks us about Katie's and my father's relationship with Linda and Sal. After Katie was found, she told police that Sal had molested and abused her. They ask my father if he knows anything about it.

"No," he says. "We don't even live there anymore. I have no relationship with them."

The man joins us in the kitchen, and we all sit around the wobbly kitchen table while she asks us further questions about Katie, John Esposito, Sal, and Linda. We say we don't know anything. My father tells them the police have already asked us these questions—*Newsday* reporters, too—and he doesn't understand why they're still asking.

The Jones Beach parking lot is packed with cars. My father carefully navigates Bobby through the rows, tells us to keep an eye out for an open parking space, slows for a family of six carrying coolers and folding chairs. The beach is cluttered with blankets and umbrellas and women in sun hats lying on their stomachs and men rubbing on sunscreen before they head into the water. My father takes off his button-down shirt and kicks off his old dress shoes, strips off his dirty jeans to reveal his black Speedo and pasty legs, which are bald below the sock line. He rubs sunscreen thickly on our arms and backs and tells us not to go too far out.

He's got his Polaroid camera. He wants my brother and me to stand beside each other in front of the water. These photos are for the judge, the lawyers, the Child Protective Services caseworkers. He takes a couple, then asks my brother to take one of him and me.

I play by myself near our blanket, shooting invisible monsters with my finger gun, doing the sound effects with my mouth. My father and brother wade in the waves up to their knees, then deeper. They call my name, gesture me to come down.

I put my imaginary fight on hold and run through the soft sand onto the harder, more stable wet sand and into the water.

"Not too far out," my father warns us as he floats.

We're two hundred feet from shore. My brother dunks his head. I do the same.

"This is fun, right?" my father says.

He asks us a lot if we're having fun. He wants to make sure we're having more fun with him than with our mother. We both tell him it's fun.

My brother swims deeper still. I follow until we're thirty yards out, maybe more.

The waves take hold of us. Pull me out farther. I giggle. Waves rock up to my neck. I wipe my eyes, and it burns.

I hear my father yell.

"Stevie, you're too far!"

My brother looks like he's laughing, but I can't tell. He's even deeper than I am. My father is fifty yards away. I've been drifting away this entire time.

Sixty yards.

My father yells. "I can't see Kenny!"

I yell, "I'm here!" but the salt water floods my mouth, interrupts me. I cough. Try to swim forward and I can't. And then a giant wave crashes over me. And another. Waves like plates of glass slap against my back, shattering on my head. The water around my legs feels as heavy as mud, and I feel water burning into my nostrils.

I burst through the surface, gasping.

I look around, but I can't see them.

My daddy's heart is old. I'm scared for him. Somebody's screaming.

I'm sinking. I'm dying here. My arms are too heavy.

Where the fuck is everybody?

I burst above water again, my mouth open, my lungs straining, but I am unable to make a sound.

I feel a tug on my leg. I gasp as more water fills my throat.

Arms under my armpits.

I see clouds and sun and birds in a sky that seems to be circling me. My stomach is nauseated. I hear the roar of a motor, see red lights and sirens.

I'm lying on an orange Styrofoam board on the wet sand. Men yell and radios crackle and lights swirl against the white sand, crisscrossed by ambulance tire tracks.

A woman puts her mouth on mine and blows into it and I cough up water and vomit, embarrassed. Someone shines a light in my eyes.

Out of the corner of my eye, I see my brother on the ground, a man pumping his chest, and my father on his back beside him.

My eyes burn.

They pick up the board and move me into an ambulance. My brother and father are still on the ground. They close the ambulance door.

I wake up in the back of the ambulance, still on the orange board.

It's getting dark out.

"You doing all right?" someone asks me.

I nod. He has juice and crackers and fruit and water.

I don't want to ask about my brother and my father because I don't want the answer.

"Your brother and grandpa are okay," he says, and I cry. I think of my father's chicken fingers and the Dunkin' Donuts napkins he saves and the time I made fun of my brother's birthmark on the back of his neck and I cry. I think about Wozels and I cry. My mother's notes in my lunch box and her smiley-face pancakes and I cry.

"You can see them soon. They're just keeping an eye on your grandpa's heart to make sure he's stable."

My throat burns when I try to talk.

"He's my dad, not my grandpa," I say.

"Oh," he says. "I'm sorry. Wow, so he's...wow, okay. Well, your dad, then."

I sit in the Coast Guard waiting room until I see headlights through a window and my father and brother getting out of a Coast Guard jeep. I walk into the lobby as they're walking in.

My father's pants are on, but his belt is undone. I hug him, and he hugs me back. I hug my brother, and he hugs me back.

"Gee, that's some shit, huh?" my father says. "I gotta sign us out, I think."

A woman has the forms on the counter.

"I didn't sign this many forms when I bought my house," he says as he goes through them, and she laughs.

We thank them and apologize and they tell us not to and we pile into the Coast Guard's jeep and the officer drives us back to our car. The parking lot is just about empty. It's dark and cold this close to the ocean. I see Bobby, old and beat-up. My father gets the screwdriver out of the glove compartment and walks quickly around to unlock our doors.

We drive in silence for minutes.

"Man, I don't think I've ever been that scared in my whole

life," he says. He wipes a tear from his face. And then he pulls the car over to the side of the road. He cries into his hands, and we cry with him. And then he says, "Listen, you guys can't tell your mother. If the court finds out, I'll never see you again. She'll take you away from me, and I don't want that to happen."

We nod.

And then he starts the car back up, flips on his left blinker, and waits for the traffic to pass before he merges back onto the highway.

chapter 8

My brother and I are standing in our backyard dressed in suits, just back from the courthouse, looking up at the sky. Sometimes, he says, during the summer months, if you look at the right time, you can see bats soar across the darkened skies. I tell him I'm scared of bats. He tells me not to be a fag. I'm wearing his old suit and his old shoes, which are too big for me and clippity-clop when I walk. My father's out having coffee with his lawyer. We've spent the past year in and out of court. The judge will grant one of my parents sole custody in the next few days. Today we sat in front of both parents, both their lawyers, a judge, a woman with a small typewriter, and a security guard in a blue uniform and answered questions. We looked at both our parents while we did it, tried to remember what they told us to say.

We go back to fantasy-casting the X-Men movie. I tell him I think Tom Cruise should play Cyclops and Arnold Schwarzenegger could be Colossus, and I want Mel Gibson as Wolverine.

"You'd never get all of them in the same movie," he says. "First of all, do you know how much it would cost? And who gets top billing? I think we should go with unknowns."

I hadn't considered any of that.

"Why did you tell the lawyer Daddy touched you?" I ask him.

He shrugs and turns away. "I don't know," he says. "Mommy told me to."

"Did he?"

"I don't know," he says. "I just said whatever would get us out of here. Aren't you tired of living in the basement?"

I'm pissed.

"At least I don't have a stupid mole on the back of my neck."

I see hurt come over his face, then quickly disappear.

"Fuck you! I'd rather have a mole than a huge ugly gap in my teeth."

"My friends like my gap," I tell him.

"What friends?"

I look at him and want to cry, and he knows it. "C'mon. What friends? Who? Wozels? She's the only one who even likes you, and that's only because she can't talk."

"Fuck you!" I say and I punch him in the arm.

He punches me back. Tells me to shut up. Calls me a faggot. I tell him to shut up and punch him back. He punches me again, harder.

I push him as hard as I can. He spits on me, and I spit back at him. Swing at him. He grabs my arms and shoves me onto the ground.

"Hit me again, you fuckin' fag!"

I get up and run into the house. He follows me in. I slam

the screen door, but he pulls it open and pins me against a wall. Tells me I hit like a girl. I struggle, but he's too strong. I knee him in the balls, then spit at him, and he punches me again and my wrist slips out of his grip and I run for the front door.

He chases me down and slams the door, tackles me, his knee in my back.

"You're so tough, right? What's wrong? C'mon."

He gets off me and walks away.

I open the closet door, grab my father's golf clubs. Pull out a 5-iron. His eyes get wide.

"No, fuck, stop . . ."

I swing at him, miss, hit the wall, the framed school photos, rosary beads, construction-paper drawings, knock them all off. Swing again. He runs into the bathroom, and I jam the golf club in so he can't close the door.

I tell my brother I hate him. I tell him I hope he dies like everyone else.

A memory. It's 1991. I'm in the living room of our old house, and I hear my mother's painful yelp from the kitchen. She screams my name. I hear dishes crashing. I run into the kitchen. My father's pushed her into the dishwasher. She's wearing her nightgown with kitty-cats on it. She grabs a knife. Swings it at him. He calls her a drunk. A cunt. Says it again. Louder this time. He wrestles her against the wall. He kicks her in the knee, grabs the knife from her. She grabs a pot of boiling water from the stove and throws it at him, hitting his neck and chest.

He screams in agony.

She runs into their bedroom. Grabs his song sheets. Tears them to shreds. Rifles through his briefcase, ripping up all his important memos. Calls him a faggot. A cocksucker. A mother-fucker. A nigger lover.

She clenches her knuckles and starts to punch herself in the arms over and over. Her skin quickly turns from a mustard yellow to a deep purplish black. She tells him she's going to call the police and show them the bruises when they get to the house.

My brother grabs the 5-iron. He's stronger than I am. He jabs the handle of the club into my ribs. I've never seen him this mad.

The handle digs into my side. I beg him to stop.

"You quit?"

"Yes," I squeal.

He gets off me and lets me up.

I stand up and look at his gloating face and smack him in the mouth. He grabs my hair and pulls me down, drags me. I tell him I hate him again, and he says he hates me, too. He says he's always hated me. He tells me I'm going to grow up to be just like our uncle Carter. Like our aunt Gina. Like all of them. A nobody. Drug addict. Junkie. Piece of shit.

My father charges into their bedroom. Grabs her by the hair and throws her down on the floor. Calls her a drunk. A cunt. He sees his briefcase open, his papers torn to shreds. He gets on top of her. Puts his hands around her neck. Tells her he's going to kill her. She screams my name. Claws his face. Grabs at his skin. Pulls his hair out.

She struggles free. My father grabs her vodka from under the bathroom sink and pours it into the toilet. She is hysterical. Throws a bar of soap at him. A toothbrush. They're fighting over the bottle when it falls and shatters on the light-blue tile.

*   *   *

I run into my brother's bedroom and grab a sack of old He-Man toys from under his bed. I pick out Skeletor and throw him against the wall. His arms and legs break off, and my brother yelps "No!" and pounds on my head. I grab the Sorceress and smash her against the wall, too, and my brother punches me in the back and calls me a faggot.

He lets go of me. Runs into my room.

"Leave my stuff alone," I cry. I run after him. He's dumped out all my Batman toys, and one by one he throws them as hard as he can against the wall. Plastic toy heads and limbs are scattered around the carpet. I jump on him, tackle him to the floor. He grabs the teddy bear I've had since I was four and I scream "No!" and he rips the bear's head off and white cotton stuffing falls out of his neck. He rams me into my small dresser, and it tips over with a crash as lamps, picture frames, change, and my Darkwing Duck underwear spill out onto the carpet.

We both jump back, scared.

"What did you do?!" he screams.

He tackles her as she tries to run out. Slams her into the hall-way wall. Puts his fist through the wall next to her. She claws his neck. He grunts in pain. They spill back into the bathroom. She pushes him into the tub, where he hits his head. She tells me to get the fuck back in my bedroom. Runs back into the kitchen, grabs the phone from the wall and calls 911, tells them my father assaulted her.

She goes into their bedroom and starts packing clothes. She's going to her sister's. Your sister's dead, *he says to her.* They're all dead. And you'll be dead soon, too. *I hear a lamp shatter. I hear it from my bedroom, where I'm trying to write in my notebook. There's a bang on the front door. My father answers. Two large, imposing cops enter. He tells them she's drunk.*

She comes out of the room crying, spitting, screaming.

The cops ask her to calm down.

How dare you take his side, you motherfuckers! *she shouts.* Oh, are you all buddies? I bet you suck each other's cocks!

You see? *he says.*

Fuck you!

They tell her again to calm down.

Fuck you, you bunch of guinea cocksuckers!

She attacks the cops, slapping and punching at their shoulders. I watch from the hallway as they wrestle my mother to the ground and drag her outside onto the front lawn, fighting them all the way.

They pull her by her hair. Cuff her wrists. Red and blue police lights flash with no sound. I run to my mother with my plastic He-Man sword. My father yells at me to get back inside. I hit the cops with the sword, screaming at them to leave her alone. My father grabs me and carries me inside as the cops drag her into the back of their car and slam the door.

My brother asks me if I quit, and I say yes.

He gets off me. His neck is scratched and bleeding. My head hurts. My arms are bruised. I'm thirsty. He goes into his room, and I stand and look at the destruction. My toys are in pieces, my teddy bear is headless. And my sadness turns again to rage and I run back down the hall and bang on his locked door until I dent the wood, the sides of my fists turning purple from the bruises. Grab the 5-iron and swing it at his door. Run into the kitchen and get a large can of Franco-American tomato sauce and chuck it down the hallway, where it cracks the door, which swings open.

"Kenny, what the fuck are you doing?!"

I run and grab another can. This time it's clam chowder. And I chuck it at him, and he leaps to avoid it. The can smashes his toe, and he yelps in pain. He sounds hurt, and I run to him, scared. His toe is bleeding. He's crying, and I never see him cry. I touch his back, and I ask him if he's okay. He doesn't answer. I tell him I'm sorry. I'm so sorry, I say. I'm so sorry.

He looks at me, turns, and smashes me in the mouth with his fist, launching me backwards into the hallway. I get up and pick up the tomato sauce again and throw it as hard as I can at him. He ducks, and the can goes through our bedroom window.

I am frozen in disbelief.

"Oh, shit," he says. "Daddy's gonna fuckin' kill you."

The cops sit with my father while my mother's in the back of the cop car. They know him well by now. They're here almost every week. They ask him what started the fight. He tells them they were watching a movie, something with Nick Nolte. She said she had a crush on Nick Nolte. My father got jealous. Called her a cunt. She left the room. Poured herself a drink. Then another. And another. And another. She threatened to call the nursing home where we sang songs to tell them he molests children. He threatened to kill her if she did.

She shouldn't be around your sons, *one cop says.*

You can't live like this, *the other says.* Being with a person like that, it's like being a hostage.

I don't want to leave my kids, *he says.*

Fight for custody, *they tell him.*

We're going to take her to the station until she sobers up, *they go on.* But then there's nothing else we can do.

You can't arrest her? For hitting a cop?

Is that what you want?

No, *he says.*

I hear the violent stutter and choke of Bobby's exhaust pipe as my father pulls into the driveway. He walks in the door and sees the carnage in the living room.

"Guys?"

"In here!" my brother yells.

I hear his footsteps in the hallway.

"What the fuck happened in here? You guys okay?"

He barges into my brother's bedroom. Sees the glass.

"What the fuck happened?"

"We got into a fight and Kenny threw a can of Franco-American tomato sauce at me and I ducked and it went through the window."

"How am I gonna...I can't pay for this shit...Stevie...I live on food stamps. I can't be replacing windows."

"*Me?* What about *him?!*"

"Him, too!"

A can rolls by his foot.

"What's this now? Clam chowder? Gee, I leave you guys home for a fuckin' hour and you destroy the house. Why don't you just burn it down next time?"

He tells me to go to my room.

"Bye, dicksucker," my brother says.

"Stevie, goddamn it, don't let me hear another fuckin' word!" my father says.

"He started it!"

"I know you antagonize him!"

"Fuck you!" my brother says to him. My father tells him to stay in his room for the rest of the night. Hours earlier my brother looked him in the eye and told the lawyers about Sal and Linda, about the basement we live in, about the food stamps, about the near drowning. And when the lawyer asked who he wanted to live with, he said my mother, and my father looked down at the table.

I hear my father's heavy footsteps in the hallway in the early morning. My mother's back from the precinct, and she punches through the glass of the back door and gets it open. He tries to slam it shut on her, but she's already inside. This is my fucking house, *she screams. He runs to call the cops again. She grabs the phone, smashing it into pieces on the kitchen floor. My mother storms into their bedroom. She's screaming that the cops raped her. My father quietly opens my door and comes inside.*

He sits on my bed.

I pretend to be asleep.

I can hear him crying.

My mother barges in, turns on the light. I open my eyes. She shows me her crimson hand, blood dripping down her wrist. Look at what your father did to me, *she screams. He wrestles her out of the room.* You see? *she yells. I hear them yelling through the walls. She calls the police again, and they come back. She's screaming again that he hit her. The cops take my father aside.*

You're going to arrest me? *he asks.* She's a goddamn drunk. You're gonna believe her? You're gonna let her stay here with my kids?

She's saying you caused those bruises. We have to arrest you.

She punched herself in the arms. I didn't do that.

My father turns around, and they cuff his hands. I watch them put him in back of the cop car. The neighbors are back out on their lawns. My mother screams from the front porch. The cops tell her to get back inside.

The next morning I wake up, and my father is sitting on my bed. He asks me if I'm okay, and I say that I am. He tells me I'm a good boy. He says they weren't fighting because of me. My mother is awake. Sober. She's making bacon and pancakes with smiley faces because she knows I love them. We sit down at the kitchen table. The leg of the table is taped at the top joint with brown duct tape. The broken plates are in the garbage pail.

You shoulda heard what Regis said. They had what's-his-face, from the cannibal movie. Hoskins.

Anthony Hopkins, *he tells her.*

He's a sweetheart, *she says.*

My father drinks his coffee. I liked him in *The Elephant Man.* Good picture.

He tells her they're out of instant coffee. She says she'll pick some up at the store.

My brother sits beside me, and we eat our breakfast as a family. We never talk about the night before.

I lie in my room in the dark. I can hear *Jeopardy!* on the TV in the other room. I open the door and make my way down the hall to my brother's room, the floor creaking as I go.

My father calls out, "Ken, where you going? Don't go starting anything!"

"I'm not," I say.

My brother sees it's me and gestures for me to come in. There's a cold draft from the broken window. I see his He-Man toys still in pieces on the floor. I sit down next to the bed on the floor.

I ask him what he's doing, and he says he's reading. John Grisham again. I ask him if we can be friends again, and he says "Okay, whatever." Tells me to be quiet, he's trying to read. And then he explodes into laughter.

"What?" I ask.

"I can't believe you attacked me with clam chowder," he says. I start to laugh.

"You should have heard your voice when I punched you in the face," he says, then he mimics me in a high-pitched British accent.

"I'm dying, I'm dying…"

"Why is my voice always British when you do me?"

"Because you're gay," he says.

"Daddy was so pissed," he says. We laugh. We're friends again.

In a few days my father will receive a phone call from his lawyer telling him he's lost custody, and he'll pick us up from school and tell us. And then he'll drive us to a Sears parking lot, where he'll give us to our mother while two police cars look on. While we wait for them to arrive, we'll sit in the mall parking lot in silence and he'll hum the melody of an old love song, then he'll look at his watch and say, "This is torture," then go back to tapping the steering wheel. He'll tell us he's very old, and he'll kiss our faces as though it's the last time. And then we'll say good-bye.

My brother and I lie silently together. Still.

"Do you really think I'll grow up to be like Uncle Carter?" I ask him.

"No," he says.

I stare up at the ceiling.

"Me, neither."

chapter 9

Helicopters fly overhead, kicking up dust and sand and small bits of pebbles as I walk Wozels along the canal. I squint upward into the bright wideness of the Arizona sky as the black chopper blades slice through the air with a machine-gun stutter.

I tug on Wozels's leash, and we head through a dirt field and over a small hill and across the street onto a mile-long greenbelt lined with electrical towers. The helicopters swarm around a tower toward the end.

Some kids are chasing the choppers on their bikes. I tug at Wozels again, and we chase after them. A middle-aged man walks out of his house barefoot and down the warm concrete sidewalk toward the tower. Little kids, too, now. Dozens of people.

Up close the tower looks to be a mile high in the air, the top well into the clouds. There's a sign on the fence: HIGH VOLTAGE—DANGER—KEEP OUT. A woman stands beside me, craning her neck. I ask her if she knows what's going on.

"They're saying a little boy climbed to the top," she tells me. "They think he might be autistic."

Suddenly another boy, a teenager, runs to the tower and starts to climb it. Parents and strangers and neighbors yell at him to get down, but he keeps climbing, swinging his leg over each new steel level as though he were hauling a bag of wet laundry. He's twenty feet high, then fifty feet high, and a man says the rush of wind from the helicopter will knock him off, but it doesn't.

He's at seventy feet and continuing to crawl into the sky. I can barely watch. My stomach feels hollow, and I wait for him to come crashing down, but he doesn't. Ignoring the voices and the winds and the enormous height, he reaches the top. The two boys are alone on top of a tower charged with 230,000 volts of electricity.

A channel 5 news van arrives. More police, who set up barricades. I look behind me and see that the greenbelt is full of people, must be hundreds of them, all looking at the sky.

In the distance, I hear, "New York!"

Shit.

I turn around and see some of the kids I know from school. I'm wearing corduroy pants, and I know they're going to make fun of me for it and I wonder if there's still time for me to run home and change my pants, borrow a pair of my brother's, but they've already seen me.

They bike over to me.

"What's up, dude? This your dog?"

I nod and kneel down beside her.

"Say hi, Wozels," I say and wave at them with her paw. They kind of laugh, and that makes me feel cool.

"This is some crazy shit, huh?"

"Yes."

"It's on the news and shit," the blond one wearing the backwards hat says. "I guess he's autistic."

They stand there, and for a minute I feel like I'm one of them. A man sees us there, and I wonder if he thinks I'm a part of the group. I do my best to enjoy the moment.

"Nice pants, New York," the boy with braces and the bowl cut says.

"Yeah. I don't know what my mom was thinking." I shrug.

"Your mom buys your pants, dude?"

"Leave him alone," says Brian, the black kid in the long basketball jersey. "Who cares about his pants?"

I've seen him around before, even talked to him once or twice. Everyone knows Brian. And for some reason he's sticking up for me.

"We're just fucking with you, dude," an older boy with red hair says. "We're taking off."

"I'm gonna stay," Brian says.

They do the chin-up, head-nod salute to one another and ride off on their bikes.

Brian stands beside me. We stare at the sky together, watch these two boys straddle a narrow metal landing a thousand feet in the air. I've never had a friend before, and I'm pretty sure I'm going to say something stupid and fuck it up.

"Wouldn't it be funny if one of them whipped out his dick right now and started pissing on everybody?" he says.

I laugh.

"Who's the kid who climbed up after him?"

I shrug.

"The news is saying it's his older brother," a woman next to us says.

I look up at the two of them. The autistic boy is frozen on the edge, and his brother is inching closer to him, trying to keep him from falling. Helicopters still circle in the distance.

An hour later, the sun has retreated behind the mountains, but the two boys are still stranded a hundred feet in the air, on top of the tower. Brian and I are hungry, and we walk through my complex to get to my apartment. The voices of young children are scattered throughout our apartment complex, through the courtyard, laughing and yelling.

I walk Wozels up the concrete steps, and Brian parks his chrome bike on the small patio space outside our front door. I open the door and let Wozels in.

"Mom, I'm with a friend!"

My brother's watching TV, looks over at me, confused. I present Brian as though he's a new car on a game show. I've never had a friend over before.

"Where's Mommy?" I ask him.

He shrugs. Wozels goes over and sits by him, and he gives her a pretzel.

We hear yelling coming from her bedroom. Crying. I look at Brian and at my brother.

"Is she crying?"

The bedroom door opens, and my mother comes barreling out into the living room with tears streaming down her red face.

My brother stands up. "What happened?"

"Your goddamn idiot uncle was arrested for robbing a goddamn bank, the fucking moron!" she says. "That was your bitch grandmother on the phone. I said to her, 'What the fuck is he robbing banks for? Probably to buy his fucking booze and drugs!' And you should have heard her on the phone. Like it's no big fuckin' deal. *Calm down, dear.* Why don't *you* calm down? I said. Better yet, why don't you go die? Everybody else is dead in this family except that old, no-good, senile, crazy fucking bitch."

The room is quiet.

"Mom, this is Brian," I say softly.

"Hi, Mrs. New York," he says.

"Oh, hi, sweetie. I'm very sorry, but my mother's a bitch. Are you boys hungry? I made tuna salad, and I have plenty."

"I'm good," he says. I say I'm fine, too.

The local TV news is showing the boys on top of the tower. My brother turns it up.

"We were just down there," I tell them.

The news confirms that the boy on top of the tower is autistic and that it's his older brother who climbed up after him.

My mother asks Brian if he has any siblings, and he says he has an older brother.

"I wish I had a brother who'd climb a fucking tower to save me," my mother says. "Wouldn't that be nice? Instead of robbing banks and getting high?" She points to the TV. "That's what brothers are supposed to do."

An hour later Brian and I go back to the tower, making our way through swarms of people, and find a place to sit together on the grass. We make small talk, and I still don't really know why he's hanging out with me. I hope someone else from school sees us together and mistakenly thinks I'm cool, too, but I don't see anybody I recognize. I want to say something funny to make him laugh, but I don't have the balls.

The crowd is hushed. A fireman has started to climb up

the tower. And another. The boys are drenched in fluorescent light, huddled together, holding on to each other. The firemen get halfway up, and the audience begins to applaud. On one side, a giant crane stretches to the sky. The two firefighters reach the top, and the crane cranks and moves closer to them. Both boys put their arms around one of the men's necks, and one of the firefighters wraps a harness around the older brother, then the younger boy, and as the crane starts to descend the audience erupts, hollering and honking horns and piercing whistles and camera flashes all around me. And I feel tears well up in my eyes, tickle my eyelashes, and I blink to let them fall down my cheeks. Soon they're halfway down, the two boys with their arms wrapped around each other, moving slowly until they're gently brought back down to earth, where paramedics wait with blankets to cover the boys and take them to safety.

Brian and I run after them, through the crowd, between the cars.

A reporter is interviewing one of the firefighters, whose face is shiny with sweat.

"The older brother is the hero here," he says. He says the brother was scared of heights but went up anyway. I think about the two of them, stranded up there, surrounded by high voltage, clinging to each other, and there's something about it that makes my breath catch in my throat.

And then I realize the older boy probably knew all along he couldn't save his brother himself. He just didn't want him to be alone.

Brian and I walk down the dark canal together and talk about how crazy the whole ordeal was.

"That was sick!" he says, and I've never heard that

expression before and I'm not even sure what it means, but I repeat it. "Yeah," I say. "So sick."

He asks me about my uncle, and I tell him I don't know much about it.

"He seriously robbed a bank?" he asks. "Is he crazy?"

"I don't know," I say.

We arrive at his house, and it's nice and big in a good neighborhood and he asks me if I want to come over tomorrow and try out his trampoline and I say yes. And then he says he'll see me at school, and I wonder if he'll say hi to me in front of everyone else.

It's late April, almost the end of the school year, and I'm heading home from school, squinting and trying to shade my face from the oppressive Arizona sun.

A horn honks behind me. I turn and see my mother's car.

My brother's at the wheel. I've never seen him drive before, and I laugh. He looks like a grown-up. And then I see Wozels's panting face peek out from the backseat.

"Get in," he tells me.

We drive around blasting music. Guns N' Roses. "Paradise City."

"Does Mommy know you have the car?" I yell.

"What?" he yells over the thumping bass.

"Turn it down!"

"Don't touch it. Speak up!"

"I said . . . never mind. Where are we going?"

"Flagstaff," he says. He says he wants to see the school he'll be going to, walk around. "Do you want to come, or do you want me to drop you off at home?"

It's a three-hour drive, and my brother takes the opportunity to sing along to the entire Guns N' Roses canon to me, starting with the songs on *Appetite for Destruction*. He does it all—vocals, guitar, drums, bass. Some parts he rewinds to do over if he doesn't care for his first take.

The car winds around a narrow mountain. Red sun slants in through the windshield. We've moved on to Billy Joel. The steering wheel is a piano. "Scenes from an Italian Restaurant."

"Are you gonna do the Brenda and Eddie part?" he asks me with pleading eyes.

"No," I say.

We swerve around the winding mountains of northern Arizona. It's getting dark, and there are no lights on the mountains and no guardrails, and sometimes he brakes suddenly when we can't see what's in front of us. Wozels is curled up and asleep in the back. Now and then she paws at me for a snack, and I give her one of the biscuits we keep in the glove compartment.

We stop and load up on candy bars and sodas and some more treats for Wozels. About an hour later and we see the sign for Flagstaff. Roads lined with tall, steady pines. And soon we enter the small town, where we're greeted by a red neon Denny's sign. A Sizzler. A Pizza Hut.

He stops the car when we get to the university, and we get out. I grab Wozels's leash, and we walk her through campus. It's colder up here. The air smells fresher, too.

"You excited?" I ask my brother.

"Yes," he says. And then he tells me that we have to call our mother and tell her we're all right. We find a pay phone, and when she picks up I can hear my mother's voice blaring on the other end.

"That bitch grandmother of yours...I'm not yelling... You're just like your prick father!"

My brother hangs up.

"Good luck with that!" he says to me. "You excited for it to be just you and Mommy?"

There are fliers on the corridor walls for parties, and we explore the dorm halls and the common rooms, where college kids play Ping-Pong and lounge around on beat-up old couches. Wozels sniffs everything. On the other side of campus, my brother wanders through the bookstore just before it closes while I stay outside with Wozels.

We drive home together in silence and through blackness, the radio stations just crackling static in the mountains.

"Seriously, though, what the fuck are you going to do, just you and Mommy?"

"You sound happy about it," I say.

"You're gonna miiiissssss me," he says in a singsong voice. "You love me. You can say it."

"No," I say and try not to laugh, and he knows it.

"Love that Joker!" he says, quoting Batman, and I burst into laughter. "Do you realize how lucky you are to have an older brother as awesome as me? Seriously, though, I can't wait to get away from all the crazy shit."

We pull into our complex. Wozels jumps out of the backseat and extends her body into a big stretch, backward and forward. Our feet are loud and clunky on the concrete steps up to our apartment.

We hear Blood, Sweat & Tears through the open window.

"Oh, great," my brother says.

Inside, the TV's on mute, and my mother is passed out on the couch.

"Mom? You okay?" my brother asks, nudging her.

"What the fuck is it?" she says. Her eyes adjust, and she

gets her bearings. "You're home safe. Okay, good, I was getting worried. Fuckin' wackos on the road. Crazy motherfuckers and old snowbirds who don't know how to drive."

She asks him where she is, and he tells her she's in the living room.

She tries to stand and can't.

"Give me your arm, Kenneth," she says, and I extend it and help her up. She goes into the kitchen, where I hear the slam of the cupboard door beneath the sink. She walks back to the couch with a full glass and sits.

"Why are you sitting here in the dark?" my brother asks her. "You okay?"

She starts crying, twisting up her face.

"Your uncle Carter died," she says, her voice breaking.

"What happened?" he says.

"Your crazy bitch grandmother found him in his room. Who the fuck knows? He was thirty-seven fucking years old, goddamn it!"

We found out later he overdosed on drugs in the bedroom he grew up in. They found pills on the table and empty booze bottles on the floor and small Baggies of powder in the dresser drawer next to a Bible and some letters from his father he never threw away. The trial for his bank robbery had been approaching.

She sits back down on the couch with a thud.

"He loved you boys very much," she says. "I know he was a dope, but he loved you. Remember how he taught you how to play the spoons on your knee?" she says to my brother. "My father should have sent him to fucking boarding school and said, 'Be a man!' Sitting around his mother's house at thirty-seven doing his fucking drugs."

"I'm sorry," I say and I kiss her warm, wet face.

"I know you are, sweet boy. Where'd your brother go? Is he having his period again?"

"I'm right here," he says.

"Yeah. You can be nicer to your mother, okay?" she says.

"Do you want to go into your room?" I ask her.

No, she says. She wants to sleep right here.

The next night, our living room is in semidarkness when I bring my dinner plate out of our bedroom and into the kitchen. My mother's sorting through old home movies next to a small, dated projector she found in storage and had my brother help her set up. Wozels sniffs the projector, and my mother tells her to stay away. We sit together cross-legged and face the projector toward a blank hallway wall.

It makes a sound like an old motor, then moving images appear, faded and grainy against the wall. My grandmother dressed for church. My dead grandfather in a suit beside her. My dead aunt, just a child with bows in her hair, scampering behind them, and next to her, my other dead aunt, even younger, in a floral dress.

"Oh, look at my Gina," my mother says and takes a sip.

Wozels walks through the beam of the projector, and my mother tells her to move. My uncle Carter comes into the frame, a chubby little boy in a striped shirt with chocolate on his fingers. He's blonder. Maybe ten years old. My age. He smiles with round cherub cheeks, and I remember my brother's voice—*You're gonna grow up to be just like him*—and see my uncle as a boy in front of me, his whole life ahead of him, smiling, laughing at the camera and pointing, and waving good-bye.

chapter 10

Second semester, seventh grade, and I'm wearing my Wozels T-shirt. My locker combination is scribbled in my mother's handwriting on a torn corner of loose-leaf paper. The two-minute warning bell sounds, and the kids scatter. Some kid comes up to me, a ninth grader with a mustache, and says, "Hey, dude, nice shirt!" I know he's teasing me so I try to walk past him, but his two friends stand in front of me.

"Yeah, dude, so, like, did your mom buy that for you after you told her you were gay?"

And then they all high-five.

Later that day, in third-period gym class. I undress in front of other boys and do it quietly and strategically, wiggling out of my corduroy pants to reveal a pair of X-Men tightie-whities.

"Nice undies, dude," says the kid to my right.

I look around.

Everybody else is wearing boxer shorts.

Everybody.

Checkered ones and striped ones and cool skater brands

like Joe Boxer and Volcom. And I'm wearing tightie-whities with a colorful photo of Professor X in his wheelchair shooting a blue laser beam out of his forehead.

And then the kid says, "Dude, it's cool. I used to wear cartoon undies, too...all the time...in third grade!"

And then they all high-five.

The next morning I arrive at school in my band shirt carrying my trombone case.

Outside the band room, some chubby kid whom I've actually seen get teased by the same kids who tease me comes up and tries to steal my trombone. He grabs the case and tries to pry it from my hands.

"Why do you even want it?" I ask him in a strained grunt as I keep my hands locked around the handle, but he's too strong and he gets it from me and runs off with my rented instrument.

It's not even 8:00 a.m., and I've already had my trombone stolen. I fucking hate seventh grade.

I walk to first-period math and sit in my chair with my head down and wait for the morning announcements. A cheery voice comes on, and we all stand with our hands over our hearts and recite the Pledge of Allegiance, then I sit and listen to the announcements—the bake sale, the assembly this afternoon for ninth graders, and Kenneth Porpora, your trombone was found in the girls' second-floor bathroom; you can come pick it up at the office.

I arrive home to a waggedy-tailed Wozels. My mother's watching *The Rosie O'Donnell Show*. She's happy today.

"Hey, baby boy, how was school?"

"Fuck that shit!" I say.

"I don't know where you learned to say *F*," she says. "You live with your prick father for a few months, and it's *Fuck this* and *Fuck that...*"

I hook Wozels up to her leash. It's time for her afternoon walk. I'm sad, and she can tell. She can always tell when I'm sad.

"You know you can talk to me," my mother says. "I am your mother."

I look at her, and I can feel the warmth of the tears in the back of my head and I want to tell her I was the only one who didn't get invited to the coolest party of the year and that they make fun of my Wozels T-shirt and they tease me because of the gap in my teeth and because I talk with an accent and because I wear the cheap jeans from Kmart. I want to tell her that I'm tired of not having any friends, and I want to break into pieces. "It's nothing," I say. "Just a lot of math homework."

"More math?" she asks with wide eyes. "Jesus Christ. What's this woman's problem? She's probably mad because her husband hates her, and she's taking it out on you."

I tell her I'm going to take Wozels out for a walk.

She mutes the TV.

"Somebody teasing you, Kenneth?" she asks me.

"No," I say.

She pauses for a moment.

"You're a very special boy," she says.

My fifth-period English teacher, a meek woman with a pointy face, assigns us *To Kill a Mockingbird* over the Christmas break. We have two weeks to read it and write an essay about a character in the book we relate to and how this person changes during the course of the story.

I sit in the third row. Tim Bennett to my right.

Behind me is Brian, whom I see walking the hallways in a light-blue North Carolina basketball jersey and a matching backwards Tar Heels hat, grinning, slapping hands with friends by the locker cages—*What's up? Last night was crazy!* The jocks and the Goth kids and the skaters all love him. The math nerds and the yearbook-club virgins and the drama team girly boys, too. The teachers and the security guards, the senior athletes and their fully developed girlfriends, who get to leave campus for lunch. He's friends, real friends, with all of them.

He's a baseball star who's even better at football and the best at basketball, which gets his name mentioned in the local paper every week. The kid the high school coaches can't wait to see graduate from junior high. In his spare time he models and helps kids with special needs.

In the corner, my classmates pass notes back and forth, loose-leaf paper folded into squares and diamonds and doves and decorated with glittery pens. They whisper about a big party over Christmas break. I peek to my right and catch a glimpse of the note. It's an invitation. Two girls in the back are doling them out.

"Him?" I hear one of them ask.

"Who, Tim Bennett?"

"No. Next to Tim."

And then I hear whispering and laughter.

The first night of Christmas break I'm watching *The Wizard of Oz* on TBS next to Wozels, who's curled up in a ball.

My mother's in her chair, her feet on the ottoman, the ice cubes clinking in her glass. She thinks the Tin Man's a homo.

"Mom, can we not tonight?"

"What, are you on your fucking period? You're not going to censor me in my house, little boy. Go live with your father if you don't like it."

The Christmas party is tonight. I didn't get invited. I tell myself it's no big deal, I didn't want to go anyway, but that's not true. My feelings are hurt. After so much loss and grief in my life, I feel a new, different kind of sadness on this night: the kids at school don't like me.

The Wicked Witch of the West is cackling in her castle.

"She is *so* my sister Kerry!" my mother says.

I'm full of nervous energy, so I grab my sneakers and the dog's leash. "I'm taking Wozels for a walk," I tell my mother. Wozels perks up as I hook her leash to her red collar and we race down the steps together.

The canal behind our apartment complex is lit only by the crescent moon. As we come to the main street at the end of it, I see a kid riding his bike up against traffic. I pull Wozels away from a small cactus and watch as the kid on the bike gets closer to me.

And then I recognize him.

It's Brian.

On his way to the party.

When he sees me, our eyes meet, and he slams on his brakes, sets one foot down like a kickstand.

"Hey, New York," he says, out of breath. "What's up, dude? Why aren't you at the party?"

I pause.

"Did they forget to invite you?"

"I wouldn't say they forgot," I answer, and he nods and kind of giggles.

"What's your real name, New York?" He tells me he's sorry because we've had a few classes together but he's never thought to ask my name.

"It's Kenny," I tell him.

"They killed Kenny!" he says and laughs. "You watch *South Park*?"

"No," I say.

"Who do you hang out with?"

I look down at Wozels and think back over my last fifty weekends sitting at home, watching professional wrestling and discovering masturbation while watching scrambled pay-per-view porn, trying to make out what's happening through the squiggly lines.

I shrug, don't even bother to lie. He knows.

"You wanna come with me?" he asks. I assume he's asking me out of pity, and I wonder for a moment if he has me confused with somebody else, then I think maybe it's a ploy, a huge practical joke that involves me arriving to a chorus of laughter and pointing.

"I don't think so," I say.

"It doesn't matter if they didn't invite you," he tells me. "If you show up with me, it'll be cool."

I don't understand why he's doing this, but I'm afraid if I question it for too long I'll let the moment slip by. So I say yes, and I tell him I have to bring my dog back home and find some clothes to wear and he says okay and he rides his bike slowly beside me down the canal.

We make it through the parking lot and up the stairs to my front door.

"Wait here, and I'll be right out," I tell him.

"Can I wait inside?" he asks me.

And then through the walls, I hear my mother: "Oh, this fuckin' lion needs to grow a set of balls!"

"Nah," I say. "It's probably better if you wait here."

He nods.

Inside, I unhook Wozels and quietly thank her for being my friend all these years while I waited for a human one. I run into my room and pull off my shirt and search in the laundry basket for something clean and not dorky. I find a blue button-down shirt I like, and though it's a little wrinkled I throw it on along with my baggiest jeans.

I go through the living room and into the kitchen in search of gum.

"Where you going?" my mother asks.

"I'm going out to a party!"

"You better be careful," she yells. "Look both ways when you cross the goddamn street. Fuckin' psychos out there."

I stand on the back-wheel pegs of Brian's bike, holding onto his shoulders as he peddles through the affluent suburban streets of this gated community. The houses look like castles. Grand estates. I can hear the bass from down the block.

I'm nervous.

I've never been to a party before.

The song "Pony" by Ginuwine is emanating from the walls of one of the large two-story houses, the bass shaking the windows. Outside, red Solo cups are scattered on the lawn, where high school kids are standing around in small circles. We walk into the party together, and when everyone sees Brian, they erupt into a chorus of *What up, dude?!* immediately followed by *What the fuck is he doing here?*

"He's with me," Brian says, just like that. And that's all it takes. I'm cool. Just like that.

I walk around the party pretending to say hi to people. I fuck up a few handshakes, and when some guy hands me a beer I say no thank you and he calls me a pussy and Brian says, "He said he doesn't want one," and the subject is dropped. By midnight I've lost sight of Brian and have spent the better part of an hour listening to this kid from Guam explain Pokémon and I wonder why he got invited to this party and I didn't— but I listen anyway.

In the back room, six kids sit around a dinner plate cutting lines of cocaine and crushing methadone pills, saying something about the high of the coke and the low of the metha- done. One of them snorts a line, and the sound of the powder into his nostril turns my stomach. I close the door and walk down the hall and down the stairs and into the yard. The bass from the stereo is muffled as I stand on the patio breathing in the cool night air. I hear a basketball bounce on the pavement and turn to see Brian shooting the ball by himself. Faking out invisible players. Spinning into a layup. Doing the play-by-play by himself. He looks back to see me and nods and goes back to shooting.

"You don't get fucked up with them?" I ask him.

"Nope," he says and keeps shooting the ball.

I wait for a moment, then ask, "Why not?"

"I just don't like to get fucked up," he says.

"Yeah. Me, neither," I say. "They don't give you shit for it?"

"I don't care if they do. They won't be giving me shit when I'm in the NBA," he says. "Those fucking burnouts are going to be getting fucked up until they're thirty, still thinking it's cool. Shit depresses me. You know the types I'm talking about?"

"Yes," I say. I think I do.

"These parties always end like this. Every time."

He sets the ball down and asks me if I want to dip.

"Does that mean leave?" I ask him, and he says yes.

"Sure," I say. "Fuck yeah, let's dip."

He asks me if I want to spend the night at his house. I've never slept over at a friend's house before, but I say yes. I call my mom and make a quick stop at home to pick up my backpack and some clothes.

Brian's bedroom has a set of bunk beds and pro wrestling posters, just like mine, and we even have the same wrestling calendar tacked to the wall. He gives me some shorts and a T-shirt to wear to bed, and I climb the bright red metal ladder up to the top bunk. He gets up and puts a VHS tape into a small TV set. Hulk Hogan versus "Macho Man" Randy Savage for the WWF championship.

After we watch we reenact the match. He's Macho Man. I'm Hulk Hogan. I hate Hulk Hogan, but I let him pick.

He gives me an elbow smash, and I fall into the pile of blankets and pillows we've laid down on the floor. "Get up, Hogan!" Brian yells at me in his best Macho Man voice.

I get up. He wants to try a powerbomb, but he's not strong enough to lift me all the way, so we both fall down laughing. He climbs to the top bunk, ducking his head to avoid the stucco ceiling. It's time for Macho Man's signature flying elbow drop.

"Macho Madness! Oooh, yeahhh," he yells, then he leaps from the top bunk down onto me, his entire body weight crashing down onto my ribs. He pins me—one, two, three—and parades around with my toy championship belt before collapsing next to me.

We both lie there exhausted.

"What do you want to be when you grow up?" he asks me. "I can't decide between basketball player or actor," he says. "My dad wants me to play ball."

"Would you ever be a wrestler?" I ask him.

"Because I drop such amazing flying elbows?"

"Mmm-hmm."

"Probably not."

I tell him I'd like to be a writer when I get older.

"You write? Dude, I wish I could write."

"I thought you could do everything," I say, and he says, "Nah, I can't write to save my life."

I smile. Tell him I could help him get better at it.

He asks me if he can read something I've written and I tell him I don't let anybody read my stuff and he says, "Don't be a bitch," and so I dig into my backpack and pull out my notebook.

"Did you write that essay yet for English?"

I tell him I have.

"Let me see that," he says, and I flip through the notebook and find the essay and hand it to him.

He stares down at the pages, reading, and I can't take watching him read my writing, so I get up and start pacing.

"Are you gonna pace the whole time?"

Yes, I say.

He goes back to reading. Flips the page.

I've never let anybody read my writing before.

"This is really good," he says. "You're gonna get an A."

I say thanks with a shy smile. He asks me if I can help him write his, and I say sure.

He flips through the notebook and starts reading aloud.

"He undoes his belt and slowly lowers his jeans…"

"No no no no no!" I yell and jump on him and grab the notebook, try to wrestle it out of his hands.

He's dying laughing. Crying.

"What is wrong with you?!" he yells, still fighting me with his hands gripping the notebook.

"Give it to me!"

"You're gonna rip it!"

He tears a few pages, but I get the notebook back.

"Jeez, relax," he says. And then he picks up a piece of torn loose-leaf paper and reads it.

"…touches her taut nipple and moans, oh, yeah, just like that…"

I try not to laugh, but I can't help it.

He spends a good hour torturing me, asking me if I can write him some porn. "Seriously, dude, it was good; I wanna know what happens to that firefighter and the housewife."

"Fuck you," I say.

"Are you that desperate? Can't you jack off to HBO like the rest of us?"

Later I'm lying on the top bunk and I'm telling him why I moved to Arizona and he's cry-laughing while I recount our journey, stories of cops and my mother watching *Frasier*.

And then it's his turn.

He tells me he's adopted. He never knew his birth parents, but he thinks about them all the time, wonders what they were like.

"Are you like your mom or your dad?" he asks me, and I become quiet thinking about it. "I wonder all the time who I'm like. Or where I got certain skills from, you know? You're really lucky to know them," he says.

His adopted dad is white and Jewish, giving him full access to black jokes, white jokes, and Jewish jokes.

"You're so lucky," I say.

He knows.

Later still we play a game where we admit embarrassing things to each other, culminating in my admission that I sang "Un-Break My Heart" by Toni Braxton at my third-grade talent show.

He stares blankly at me. "Don't you ever tell that to anybody, understand?"

"What?"

"'Un-Break My Heart'?!" he shouts. "Nobody can know that."

"It's that bad? Worse than the clip-on earring?"

"Nah...nothing's worse than that," he says, then he holds his hand out and tells me he found my vagina on the floor. He thought I might want it back.

We laugh.

He says, "You're funny as hell, New York," and I'm not sure why he thinks that, but I'm happy he does.

It's almost four, and we begin to get sleepy. The conversation turns more serious, and he starts to talk about his friends and how he sometimes wonders if he has any real friends. He seems sad, and it occurs to me that we have a certain kind of loneliness in common.

"You wanna go to the mall tomorrow?" he asks me, and I tell him I do.

Brian sits beside me in fifth-period English. We joke back and forth to each other until our teacher says, "Enough, boys," and we stay quiet and try not to laugh. She says, "Would anybody like to read theirs aloud?" but nobody says anything, then Brian says, "Kenny should read his!" Then he adds, "It's actually really good." She looks at me and asks me to read it out loud, but I'm afraid I'm a bit too shy for that, so I shake my head no.

Brian puts his hand on my shoulder and whispers in my ear: "C'mon, dude."

"No," I say.

"You're a really good writer," he tells me. "Don't be so shy about it. Be proud of it."

"I don't want to."

"Don't be a bitch."

"I'm not a bitch."

And then he threatens to tell the whole class I know all the words to "Un-Break My Heart" by Toni Braxton if I don't read it.

"What?"

"Forgot you told me that, huh?"

Sure, I say. I'll read it. No problem.

I stand in front of the class. I've never read my writing for anybody before. And in a timid voice I say, "My story is about Scout's mother, who has already passed away when the book starts. We never get to meet her, but sometimes Scout has memories of her that make her sad." And then I begin to read. In my story, her mother is a funny, pretty woman, but she's sad, too, and she drinks herself to sleep in front of the television.

"They had TV during the Great Depression?" my teacher asks me, and smiles from behind her eyeglasses, and I watch her scribble something in her grade book.

Fuck. There goes my A.

She tells me to continue.

I take a deep breath, and I read my story.

chapter 11

I'm holding onto Brian as he speeds down the street on his stripped chrome bike. He bunny-hops off the curb, and we bounce. I'm sitting on his handlebars, looking out at the dark suburban road ahead of us. He steers us around the block, then takes a sharp right out of the neighborhood and onto a main road. It's a warm August night. The canal is bumpy. Potholes, pebbles, rocks.

I'm fourteen now, a little taller, and ninth grade is a different place for me as Brian's friend. Instead of hearing whispers and giggles, I walk into classrooms to see clusters of popular kids argue over who's going to sit next to me. I wear Brian's North Carolina hat every day to school, sometimes down over my eyes, sometimes backwards and a bit to the side.

The bike hits a bump, jolts, and we hit the ground stumbling off. Laughing.

"Shit, dude..."

He bunny-hops back on and idles his way toward my apartment complex.

He steers himself in figure eights, idles slow enough for me to walk beside him, and hits the brakes as we turn the corner.

"Is that my mom's car?" he asks.

It is. A huge white Cadillac parked in the reserved parking space next to my mother's.

"What the fuck? Why would she be here?" he asks.

He chains his bike on our stairwell railing and we run up the steps.

Roberta Flack's pained voice is blaring through our window screen. We hear laughter.

I open the door. Brian's mother is standing in my kitchen with a glass of wine in her hand. She's singing "The First Time Ever I Saw Your Face" with my mother. The two of them are laughing.

"Hey, baby!" she shouts when she sees Brian.

"Hey, Ken-Ken!" my mother shouts.

My mother is happy drunk.

The bass from "Papa Was a Rollin' Stone" starts, followed by some wah-wah '70s funk guitar.

"Ooh, baby, turn it up!" Brian's mom yells. Her name is Tracy. A pretty, light-skinned black woman with long hair down her back, she dresses in fancy pastels and wears long fake fingernails and perfume.

"What's going on?" Brian says.

"We're having fun, baby!" my mother says. Tracy jumps in. "That's right. A little wine. A little music. Talking about our husbands."

I've never seen my mother have a friend before. It's nice for her.

"It was the third of September..." Tracy sings along with the first line of the song.

"Ah! My birthday!" my mother shouts.

Brian's confused. "Wait, how did you even...why are you even here?"

"I was looking for your ass because you were supposed to be home at six, and I got worried."

My mother grabs Wozels by the paws and starts dancing with her. Wozels is on her hind legs, trying to keep up.

"Can I have some wine?" Brian asks.

"No! You may not, Mr. Fourteen-Year-Old."

He looks at me. "Worth a shot," he says with a shrug. "So Mom, I'm spending the night here."

"Did you ask Kenny's mom if it was okay?"

"He can stay! Everybody's welcome at my place, baby!"

"Kenny, I told your mother she should be a comedian. Has Brian told you I'm a comedian?"

"No," I say.

She swats him with the back of her hand. "You didn't tell him? Well, anyway, I act, I do stand-up, a little bit of everything. I'm trying to get your mother to come up on stage with me at the club...they'd love her."

She looks at me.

"Why you so quiet? Every time I see you you're quiet."

I shrug. "It's just the way I am."

"I'm hungry," Brian says.

"Ooh, me, too," Tracy says. "You know what I'm in the mood for? One of those Grand Slams from Denny's."

It's almost midnight. "Table for four?" asks the night-shift hostess at Denny's, grabbing a stack of menus.

We order Grand Slams and chocolate milks and coffees.

Tracy's telling a story about Brian growing up. The time he

insisted on wearing his clothes to school backwards, like Kris Kross. He had the braided hair like theirs, too, she says, trying to embarrass him.

"He looks just like you," my mother says, and Brian and Tracy start laughing.

"We adopted Brian when he was a baby," she says.

The check sits on our table for hours while we sit talking and laughing. Our mothers commiserate over motherhood and husbands; Brian and I talk about wrestling.

"Worst anniversary gift?" Tracy asks my mother.

"Oh, Jesus," my mother says. "I'm lucky I got anything. One year he bought me snow tires."

"Mmm, romantic. And..."

"One year he got me a garden hose."

Tracy screams with laughter. "That's good, I need to use that in my act."

"What do you want from me?" my mother asks. "I married old."

"I married white!" Tracy says. "And Jewish."

"I should have been smart like you," my mother says.

I get to sleep late and wake up to my mother barging into my room, yelling about the motherfucking bitch who works at the front office of our apartment complex.

"What's wrong?" I say, sitting up groggily.

"They're saying we're behind on the rent and they're evicting us. Fuckin' asshole lying pieces of shit. That fat bitch at the desk with her hair in the little bun, Miss Look-at-Me-I'm-So-Fucking-Pretty... Tells me we have thirty goddamn days to get out."

"So what do you want me to do?"

"Oh, you're a little pussy like your father!"

She slams the door.

I follow her out into the living room. I'm only wearing underwear. I hate arguing in my underwear.

"What do you want me to do?"

"Go talk to the motherfuckers!" she cries. "Tell them you're in school and you can't be evicted."

"I don't think that's going to work," I say.

"Fine. Fuck you. I'll go talk to them. God forbid I ever have a man in my life to do anything!"

She walks out the front door, slamming it behind her.

The school cafeteria is congested with teenagers carrying orange trays of burgers and fries and pizza and soft pretzels. Brian and I sit together at a table near the back. We don't have the same lunch period, but I skipped PE to sit with him.

"So I'm moving to Florida," I tell him.

"Seriously?"

I nod.

"Well, that's bullshit," he says. "You can't go."

"We're getting thrown out of our apartment, and my mom has a friend there," I tell him.

"Wait...when?"

"Soon," I tell him. "Like, we have to be out at the end of the month."

"Dude, no! What the fuck? That's like not even two weeks!"

He looks sad. I'm a little bit happy that he's going to miss me. It feels good knowing I'll be missed somewhere. But it's hard to see him so shaken up, and it occurs to me that he may not be as used to change as I am. He's so popular at school, always has so many friends around him, kids he's known longer and better, that it never occurred to me I may be his best friend, too.

"Well, we're going to throw you a big party," he says.

I smile.

And I suddenly don't want to go.

"Fuck this shit," I tell my mother when I get home. "I'm not going."

"Oh, knock it off," she says. "You going for your Academy Award?"

"I'm not leaving!"

"Then stay," she says. "Move in with your rich black friend. Maybe Tracy can come pick you up in her Cadillac. I'm sure they have plenty of room for you. Maybe she can adopt you, too."

Over the next few days I tell my teachers I'm moving to Florida. It's barely a month into the new semester, and all the projects and papers and books I'd been working on go unfinished. None of it matters now. Half-finished art projects. A clay pot in ceramics that looks more like a deformed teapot. I leave it all. Take my transcripts with me.

The interstate leading east to Florida is miles of desolate road and radio static. Wozels is stuck in the backseat next to boxes and blankets and backpacks and bags stuffed with all the clutter we've accumulated. My mother can barely see out of our back window. Wozels licks ice cubes out of my hand when she gets too hot. We play Billy Joel cassettes and pull off at truck stops that have glass cases of day-old doughnuts and cheap sunglasses on racks. I stretch and walk Wozels and grab some roast-beef sandwiches from Arby's before we get back on the road.

I imagine Florida to be beautiful. Sandy beaches and palm trees and Disney World and boy bands. I daydream with my head against the passenger-side window. The plan is to meet Nana in Florida and share a home with her. She's sold her Amityville house, which she said was too big. Too many sad memories. Too many dead children on the couches and in the bathtubs.

Our nights on this road trip are spent in whatever cheap motel allows dogs. It feels familiar to be in motels again, to swim in the pools and wander the parking lots and watch cars pass by on strange highways. It takes us three days to get to Florida.

Sarasota is muggy in August, drizzling warm rain when we arrive. The first thing we see is a main road lined with fast-food chains. My mother's not impressed.

"This is it?" she says. "It looks like Amityville."

We check ourselves into another budget motel and unload our car again. Something new breaks or bends each time we pack and unpack: an important necklace or a Christmas ornament or magazine we were trying to keep in decent condition.

We meet Nana at the airport baggage claim. She's in a wheelchair being pushed by an airline attendant.

"Oh, please," my mother says to me. "She doesn't need a fuckin' wheelchair. She needs everyone to know the queen is here."

Behind Nana is another airline attendant pushing a dog carrier. Out at the curb, we help the attendants load Nana's bags into our car. I squeeze myself into the backseat, and her new dog, Mimi, jumps into the back with me and starts licking me frantically. She tries to bark, but no sound comes out.

Another silent bark. Like a pathetic cough.

"What's wrong with Mimi?" my mother asks.

"I had her de-barked," Nana says and smiles.

"Why?!"

"Because the Italian man across the street kept calling the police because of noise complaints."

"So you had her vocal cords removed? That's sick."

"The doctor said it was painless, and I think she's happier," she says.

Mimi coughs up a few more bark attempts.

We only stay in Florida for three weeks, most of it in the motel. Nana backs out of our plan to buy a house once she realizes there are black people living in Florida. So we all move back to Arizona: my mother, Nana, Mimi, Wozels, and me in a small car packed with boxes and dog carriers and fast-food bags and Subway soda cups and blankets and beach towels.

It's a long drive home.

I call Brian from a pay phone somewhere in Texas to tell him I'm coming back.

We drive back to our old apartment and hop the patio wall and open the sliding glass door and sleep on the floor and wake up early before the maintenance men arrive to paint the walls. We move into a Best Western on Main Street next to the Wendy's. We move out of that into a rental house with Nana but move out a week later because she doesn't trust the real-estate agent due to his Italian last name, then finally we move into another apartment.

*   *   *

The school principal tells me our time in Florida caused me to miss too many days of school for me to still get credit for the school year, so I spend my freshman year going to classes I won't receive credit for. In English class I read Willa Cather, and my teacher takes me aside and tells me I should consider signing up for advanced writing classes. He thinks I have a knack for it.

Another teacher tells me about a short-story competition and encourages me to enter.

I ask Brian what he thinks, and he says, "I think you'd win," so I write a story about my father singing songs in nursing homes to dementia patients younger than he is. And when they announce the winners over the loudspeaker and my name isn't among them, Brian leans over to my desk and asks, "Are you gonna cry like a little bitch?" and I laugh and nod, then he gets serious and says, "Seriously, don't give up on it," and I say, "You're so fucking corny," and he gives me the finger.

I talk to my brother on the phone and tell him I like writing and he tells me I should read Roger Ebert and I spend my next lunch break at school on the library computer reading his movie reviews, which aren't so much movie reviews as essays about life. One of his reviews is of a Belgian film, *The Son*, about a man named Olivier whose young son was murdered and who befriends and helps the young boy responsible for the death. "You have seen the film and know what Olivier knows about this death," Ebert writes. I scribble those words into a notepad, and I continue scribbling, "*The Son* is about a man who needs no rules because he respects his trade and knows his tools. His trade is life. His tools are his loss and his hope."

I sit back and take a deep breath. I haven't seen the film, but when I get home from school I ask my mother to rent it for me. I struggle to keep up with the subtitles and the shaky camera style, and I don't always know what's going on, but by the end I think I understand what Ebert means.

I return home from school on a Friday excited about the weekend: WrestleMania is on Sunday, and my mother has agreed to order it on pay-per-view for Brian and me. I throw my backpack on the couch, grab Wozels's leash, and remind my mother that Brian will be coming over.

She turns on the faucet and starts doing dishes. Turns the water off. Wipes her hands on a dish towel. I sit down at the computer Nana bought us and look up some more of Ebert's reviews on the Internet.

"Oh," she says, "I almost forgot. The public library called..."

I freeze, suddenly remembering that I reserved a book called *'N Sync Confidential*.

My mother walks over and hands the book to me with a coy little smirk on her face. All five boy-banders are smiling big, toothy grins, with blond highlights against a neon-green backdrop, their lead singer, Justin Timberlake, in sunglasses.

"'N Sync?" I stutter. "Who would reserve this?...Super gay...Look at these guys..."

My mother just stands there with her arms folded and lets me talk myself into circles.

As it turns out, my mother had known I was gay since she first checked our computer's browser history a few months ago and found about three dozen websites dedicated to shirtless pictures of Justin Timberlake, a few virus-ridden sites of fake nude photos of Justin; gallery after gallery of Justin's face sloppily Photoshopped onto someone else's body. The photos were clearly fakes, but for me at fourteen, it did the trick.

"Who's your favorite?" my mother asks me, and I tell her I don't like any of them, but she is undeterred, and from that moment she records just about every appearance 'N Sync ever makes on a talk show, yelling, "Kenneth, your boyfriends are on TV!" whenever they appear on the screen.

When Brian arrives I answer the door, and before he has a chance to enter the apartment I tell him that the racist grandmother I'd told him about lives with us now.

"Should I tell her I'm Hawaiian?" he asks me, laughing.

Nana emerges from my mother's room, where she was finishing watching *The Birdcage*, which my mother had rented for her.

"Nana, this is my friend Brian."

"Oh," she says with a phony smile. "Isn't that nice. Dennis, is it?"

"Brian," he says.

"Diane?"

"Brian," my mother shouts. "B-B-B-B-B!"

"Oh, yes. Brian." She looks uncertain but shakes his hand.

"Kenneth, can I talk to you for a minute, please?" my mother asks. I follow her into her bedroom, leaving Brian alone with my grandmother.

"I think you should ask your friend to go," she says. "She makes me nervous. She's gonna start talking about the black woman who stole her job in 1972 . . . about how they're taking over sports—"

She's interrupted by the sound of Nana's explosive falsetto laugh through our thin walls, and we go back into the living room.

"Kenneth, did you know they did a remake of *The Nutty Professor*?" Nana says. "Dennis was telling me Eddie Murray plays all the parts. He even dresses up like a tiny Negro woman! Doesn't that sound fun?"

Brian does a perfect Eddie Murphy impression, and he stomps around my living room reenacting the dining room scene as Nana laughs hysterically.

"Well, this is new," my mother says.

Nana starts clapping. "Oh, you should be in the movies! It sounds like the movie my daughter just rented for me. What was it, dear? The one I loved?"

"*The Birdcage*," my mother says.

"Yes! *The Birdcage*. Have you seen it?" she asks Brian.

He hasn't, but Nana fills him in.

"Nathan Lane plays a homosexual man who dresses up like a woman and sings show tunes. He's married to Robin Williams. And I didn't know Robin Williams was homosexual. Did you?"

"No," Brian says.

"I guess he'd be a bear," Nana says.

"Oh, Jesus in heaven," my mother says.

"I saw a program on my morning show about the homosexuals, and they said there were animal distinctions," Nana goes on. "And one of them was bear. It means a man with a furry chest."

"Thank you, Mother. I'm going to go kill myself now."

My grandmother looks back at Brian and continues.

"Well anyway, the two gay fellows live with this flamboyant

Brazilian maid, that man from *Mad About You*, the dog walker, and he wears the craziest outfits! And they all put on a burlesque show."

She's making herself laugh reliving the film.

"Have you ever?! Well, it turns out they have a son who is marrying the daughter of a Republican! Gene Hackman." She grabs a handful of peanuts to nibble and continues talking with her mouth half full. "Once Gene Hackman gets wind of the wedding, he wants to meet the parents!"

Her eyes widen further. "But the son of the two gay men doesn't want Gene Hackman to know his parents are gay. So Nathan Lane pretends to be a woman!"

"All right Mother, come down before you have a stroke," my mother says.

"So Nathan Lane is dressed up like a woman, and they believe it. I mean, isn't that absurd?"

It's later, and the sun has gone down. The pay-per-view event is well under way, and my mother's making spaghetti and meatballs, and in a separate pan, sautéed hamburger meat she'll mix into Wozels's bowl, hoping to trick her into eating the bland dog food she's been sniffing and snubbing lately.

Nana's asleep in the chair with her stockinged feet on the ottoman.

My mother's given us blankets and pillows, and together he and I build a fort, a tent that takes over the whole living room, so big that even the TV fits beneath it, and we sit crosslegged and watch, making bets on who will win, keeping track on a piece of paper.

Wozels sticks her head into the fort and sniffs around, suspicious. The fort has infringed on the area where she usually brings her doggy treats, and when she decides to enter, she leaves only her tail outside the wall of blankets.

My mother laughs.

"Oh, you should see this! All I can see is Wozels's tail wagging! She's a riot!"

Here and there throughout the evening, my mother will come into the living room with another story.

"Did Kenneth tell you about the time we went to Amish country?"

"No," Brian says.

My mother takes out a colorful package of Kodak photos and shows him a picture of me in an Amish straw hat and a fake beard.

"Is that you?" Brian says and cracks up.

My mother shows him our happiest memories, and he makes a collection of his favorite photos. He tells my mother he's never left the state of Arizona, and she says, "You see, Kenneth? How many kids can say they've been back and forth across the country four times? Not many! You're very lucky, you know?"

As she looks through the photos, she says quietly, "We had a lot of happy times together. I hope you remember some of them."

When I tell Brian stories about my life, he sees them differently from the way I do. He doesn't see the loss. He sees the opportunity. The adventure.

In front of my mother, he says to me, "No wonder you have so many cool stories," and she says, "Thank you for saying that, Brian!"

For the first time, I start to see my life in a new way. I start to see the opportunity, too. But I'm sad as I watch my mother tell him our stories. I worry that she thinks I hate her, that I won't remember our better days, her best attempts to give me the happiest possible life.

She's got a new package of Kodak photos from the kitchen drawer.

"This is us at the Renaissance festival," she says.

"Is that you dressed as a Viking?" he asks me, and I try to change the subject.

The house is quiet, and Brian and I lie still beneath our fort of blankets and pillows. Wozels pokes her head in periodically and growls.

"I think she's jealous," Brian says.

"So what did you think of Nana?" I ask him.

"Nice," he says.

"I can't believe she loved you so much," I tell him. "You don't understand. She refuses to go to Red Lobster because they once had a black family in one of their commercials."

"What can I say?" he says. And then he says, "I like your family. They're funny."

Soon it's 2:00 a.m., and we've moved to my room; we lie together and embellish stories and trade old photographs and cover our mouths when we laugh so as to not wake my mother. I dig through my dresser and find the Wozels calendar my mother made me when I was younger; Wozels posed in a different outfit for every month—Easter bunny ears for April, a pumpkin head for October, a Santa hat for December. In one photograph, Wozels's expression is one of sheer terror as she cowers in the corner wearing a yarmulke for what must've been Yom Kippur.

"The thing is, I can actually see your mom putting the

yarmulke on her and yelling at her to stay still," he says, then mimics her voice: *Don't you move, you little motherfucker!*

We talk until the first signs of sunup, the gray blue of day-light, and we sleep through the first half of the following school day.

PART TWO

chapter 12

I stare at myself in the dirty bathroom mirror.

A crude fluorescent light buzzes. The broken fan grinds out a dusty odor. I look back at myself. Turn my face to look at the pimples clustered on my temple and cringe. I scoop the cakey black makeup out of the flimsy plastic tray and wipe a thick glob of it across my forehead. And then another across my cheek. I'm wearing a black basketball jersey. The letters B-R-I-A-N are taped to my back with silver duct tape I got out of the storage unit. Soon my entire face is black. Then I start on my arms.

I come out of the bathroom and stand before my mother. She's watching a rerun of *Frasier*. Wozels is in the corner, gnawing on her bone.

"Look at this bald asshole," she says, waving a hand at the TV. "This is comedy? I'm only watching this shit because I can't find the remote. Where's the fucking remote? I better not have left it at the crazy bitch's house."

After Nana made us leave the house that had the Italian real-estate agent she bought a small house in a retirement community, and we moved in with her. That lasted about four months, until she kicked us out after she and my mother got into a fight about Paul Reiser. Nana loves Paul Reiser, but my mother finds his voice monotone, so Nana had a marshal escort us out of her house the morning before my sixteenth birthday. The last time I saw her, she looked like a Batman villain, sporting a shaved head (because she thought mites had infested her house and body, she cut off all her hair) and a mask over her mouth. From there my mother and I spent a week in our car, then stayed at a nearby Days Inn before we found a motel room with weekly rates next door to a Pizza Hut.

My mother turns to look at me. "What the fuck is this?!"

I am completely black. My face, neck, arms, hands, legs—every bit of exposed skin is swathed with thick black paint. It doesn't look exactly like I thought it would, but it's the best I could do.

"I'm going as Brian!" I say and smile.

"You're going to get yourself killed going out like that in this neighborhood! Those fucking derelicts who hang outside the Waffle House are gonna knife you."

"They're not gonna knife me. It's a joke," I say. "Plus," I add, "I'm getting a ride."

"Oh, and *I'm* the racist?"

I turn away from her and go back into the bathroom.

"And you better not be getting black paint everywhere. I'm not paying these assholes' cleaning fees. They've already gotten enough out of me."

A car horn blares from downstairs.

"That's him," I say.

"He's gonna let you in his car like that? Bring a sheet with you."

I grab a sheet from the small cabinet and carefully kiss Wozels good-bye and run out.

Brian is standing alongside his car, leaning against the swung-open door, the radio thumping. He sees me and smiles.

"What the hell are you supposed to be?"

I turn and point out his first name on the back of my jersey.

He bursts out laughing. "Fuck," he says, looking me over. "I swear to God I almost came as you, too."

"Shut up," I say.

"I swear, dude. I had these fake teeth with a gap in the middle and blue contact lenses..."

I'm smiling.

"...and these big goofy-ass ears to go with your big head and the same jeans I've been wearing since I was six..."

I stop smiling.

"...and I had this dorky-ass WrestleMania sticker on my school binder and a high-pitched little-girl voice and a tiny dick, just like you. I swear I almost wore it."

"Fuck you," I say.

"And where's your Afro?" he asks me.

Oh, shit, I think. "I forgot it upstairs," I say jokingly and smile.

He takes off his North Carolina basketball cap and hands it to me. I put it on backwards, just as he wears it.

Cars and trucks are parked all along the road as we approach the party. Brian finds a spot, and we approach the house together. Some generic hip-hop album is blasting. On the walls I see handsome family photos, including several of the kid throwing the party. I don't know him. There must be two hundred high school kids here, some older. Boys with braces and acne in backwards hats and fifteen-year-old girls with makeup and cleavage. Everyone nods at us as we come in.

"What the fuck are you supposed to be?" some drunk girl slurs. I walk past her, regretting my costume as I squeeze through the crowd, trying not to get black paint on anyone. We find our friends in the small backyard, which smells like spilled beer and weed.

"Brian!"

They greet him with high-fives and chest bumps, but they don't acknowledge me at first.

"Oh, shit! I didn't even recognize you, dude!" my friend Jeff exclaims.

"Oh, shit!" echoes another. "What are you supposed to be?"

I turn around and show them the name on my back.

They erupt in stoned laughter.

"Dude! Dusty, c'mere, dude. Kenny came as the black man."

Our friends laugh when they see me. They all want photos, and we take turns posing.

"Cameron! Dude, check it out. There's two Brians!" Jeff says.

Brian and I take photos with each other. Arms slung around each other's shoulders. Back-to-back. Smiling in all of them.

Inside the house I find the bathroom door and bang on it. Some guy I don't know opens it a crack and tells me to fuck off before slamming it shut. Jeff tells me that guy's name is Casey and he's a senior at another school and he's fingering his girlfriend in there. He says it with a big Cheshire-cat grin and proud, wide eyes.

"Awesome," I say.

"Have you seen Brian?" I ask him.

He hasn't.

I knock on one of the bedroom doors, and some red-eyed kid opens it as pungent smoke pours out of the room and all around me. He asks me what I want, then I hear Brian say, "He's cool," and the kid lets me in. Brian's sitting with a tall, colorful bong, and he flicks the lighter and he lights the bowl and sucks and the bong bubbles and he blows smoke out into the room. I step over legs and feet in skater shoes and make a space for myself next to Brian.

Some kid I don't know hands the bong to me, and I pass it to my left.

"Hit that shit," he says in a choked voice.

"He doesn't get high," Brian says.

"No shit?" the kid says.

"Never seen him drink, ever," Brian says.

"How come?"

I shrug. "I don't know."

"How do you guys know each other?" he asks Brian. Brian tells him we've known each other forever, that I'm his best friend.

I tell Brian I'm going to head home. I look around the circle at these burnout kids passing their bong around, and Brian and I share a look.

"You coming?" I ask, and he shakes his head, tells me to find another ride home.

I jump out the back of the pickup truck and thank the two random guys from the party for the ride home. I walk up the motel steps to our room, tap softly on the door, then open it with my key card. My mother is asleep in her nightgown with a late-night rerun of *Roseanne* playing, one of the Halloween episodes. Wozels is all over me, sniffing my legs, her tail sweeping the edge of the bed and thudding against the leg of the circular table in the corner. She wants to go out. Gives me a polite warning growl. I grab her leash and say "Shh" so she doesn't wake my mother.

"Fucking buncha bullshit ripoff motherfuckers," my mother blurts out in a broken mumble. She must be dreaming, because she goes right back to her soft, throaty snore.

I hook the leash onto Wozels's collar and grab the key card.

Our lonely side street is desolate. Across the street is a boarded-up gas station and a strip mall with a Waffle House and a storefront that sells bongs and dildos. A brightly lit Burger King. A bookstore with a GOING OUT OF BUSINESS banner strung above its door. On the corner, a drunk homeless man sits on the curb. And some loud teenagers. Black and Hispanic and white wannabe thugs wearing tattoos and wife-beaters. Their girlfriends in gold chains. They see me painted black. Ask me what the fuck I'm supposed to be.

I ignore them, focus on Wozels.

They yell after me, calling me a faggot. I don't look back. I pull Wozels down another side street and away from them.

She sniffs a patch of grass, and I daydream about being a rock star. I have long hair and I play lead guitar and it's just a small band of four and they can't replace me. The four of us do everything together, laugh on tour buses and eat together at diners and know that someday these will be the times we will remember forever. I have full conversations with my bandmates in my head. They never have faces, but I know who they are.

I glance over at Wozels, who's circling and sniffing, and I give her a slight tug.

"Come on, buddy," I say, but she resists. She squats down to pee, and when she gets up, she stumbles, woozy-legged. Stumbles again.

"No," I say.

And then she collapses onto her right shoulder and onto the ground.

"No!" I scream and run to her, drop to my knees, touch her side. Her eyes are wide. Her chest is heaving.

"No, no, no."

I pick her up, cradling her neck, and I run. I run down this barely lit alley and back onto the lonely side road and past those motherfuckers who laugh at me again and I let my tears fall out of my eyes and bleed into the paint on my face. The night blurs past me and I beg God for help and tell Wozels she's going to be just fine, *It'll all be okay, you're okay, just please, please, hold on,* and I tell God I'm sorry for everything I've ever done and run into our parking lot and up our steps, kick the bottom of the fucking door, and scream for my mother.

"Help me!" I wail.

I have to set Wozels down on the pavement to dig into my pocket for the key card.

"Mom! Help me!" I scream again.

I swipe the card and get a red light.

"Help me!"

She opens the door.

"What are you screaming like that for?"

She's annoyed until she sees Wozels on the ground. "What happened?"

I pick her up and carry her inside, hysterical.

"She collapsed," I wail. "I don't know. She just fell. We have to bring her to a doctor."

"I'm not going to the vet with you in blackface, for Christ's sake!"

"She's gonna die!" I scream at her.

My mother knows Wozels is dying, and her face looks like it might shatter into pieces.

"Okay," she says. "You're going to have to drive."

I don't have a license, and I've only driven in circles in church parking lots with friends. My mother puts a coat over her nightgown and slips on her shoes and I pick up Wozels again and we rush downstairs and into the car.

"Drive careful," my mother warns me. "There're fuckin' cops everywhere."

I start the car and put it in reverse. Back out slowly. Pull out of the motel and get onto the main road. I wipe tears from my eyes and get black paint on my shirt and on the steering wheel and my mother tells me to focus on the road. She tells me Wozels has lived a good life, and I tell her to shut up, to not talk like that. I pull onto the highway and drive slowly in the right-hand lane until I pull off at the exit my mother points out. I wait at the red stoplight and stare up at it, the pixilated color melting into my burning tears, and I can barely see.

"Come *on*!" I scream, pounding my fists on the steering wheel. "Fuckin' light!"

The light turns green, and I make a quick left.

"Is she okay?" I ask, and my mother looks back and says she's the same, hasn't moved. She reaches back and pets her softly.

"Sweet girl, we're going to make you feel better," she says.

I pull into the twenty-four-hour urgent-care parking lot and park crookedly and jump out of the car. I pick up Wozels, who's breathing heavily, and run her inside into a waiting room that's empty except for the receptionist.

I tell her I need help, and she looks like she doesn't know what to say.

"Please!" I scream at her. "My dog collapsed while I was walking her."

She rushes around and kneels beside Wozels, who's lying on the cool tile floor of the lobby.

"Okay, okay. When did this happen?" she asks.

"About fifteen or twenty minutes ago."

"Okay, and how old is she?" she asks.

"She'll be thirteen soon," I choke out, and I know that means she's old and I knew she was getting old and every night before bed I'd tell myself she wasn't old and she had plenty of time left.

Another woman in a white coat helps her pick Wozels up, and they tell us they're going to bring her into the back.

Wozels looks scared. I kiss her on the face and tell her it's going to be okay. My mother kisses her, too, and tells her we'll be waiting for her outside.

We wait in the turquoise cushioned chairs in the lobby. My mother rubs my back and in her quietest voice tells me she's sorry. She calls me sweet boy and tells me Wozels is going to be okay. She tells me I've been a wonderful friend to Wozels. Tears fall onto my lap and dot my dirty blue jeans. She hands me a tissue.

"The whole time you were driving I was just praying we wouldn't get pulled over," she says. She starts to giggle a bit.

"What?"

"I just pictured your mug shot, looking like this."

I smile.

"Remember the first time Wozels saw herself in the mirror?" she asks me.

"Yeah," I say. "And she couldn't stop barking and every time she barked she thought another dog was barking at her and she'd tilt her head, confused."

"Or how she used to watch the dogs on Animal Planet and check behind the TV for them?"

"Yes," I say. And then my laughter turns back to tears and she rubs my back and tells me again it'll be okay.

The vet comes out. A weathered-looking woman in her forties with a gruff voice. She asks us to come into the back. We follow her into a small, sterile room, where Wozels is lying on a bench, still on her side.

"Hi," I say, and give her a kiss. "Are you okay?"

I look up at the vet.

"I wish I had better news," she says. "There seems to be a mass in her stomach about yay big"—she extends her hands to the size of a football—"and we think it's likely cancer."

I stare at the ground.

My mother's eyes go wide and turn watery and her mouth turns down. She turns her face away from me.

"How long does she have?" I ask.

"I'd say it's a matter of months," the vet says.

"Months?" My voice cracks in disbelief.

"You're gonna kill him?" my mother says, pointing at me.

"Well, I'm not going to lie to him," the vet answers.

"Is she in pain?" I ask.

The vet tells us the mass could have developed in the last few months and is likely pressing on her bladder and causing her pain. She has pain medication she can give us. She also tells us they can operate, but at her age it's a risk. It's a sixteen-hundred-dollar operation with no guarantees. My mother says we can't afford it. I think of ways to get money. Illegal ways. I don't care.

The vet says she's very sorry. She gives us some pamphlets and tells us to bring her back and they'll run some tests and X-rays and find out more. We nod and say thank you, and I hoist Wozels gently into my arms, as though she were a baby, to take her home.

My mother drives home while I stare out the passenger-side window. She helps me carry Wozels up the stairs and softly lay her on the bed.

"Aww, my sweet little girl," my mother says and pets her ears.

I walk into the bathroom and pull off my clothes and step into the small shower and turn the water on. Step out. Wait for it to heat up, then step back in. Stand under the weak stream of water and let it wash the black paint off me. It runs off my body and pools around my feet, looking like dirty watercolors before it goes down the drain. I sit down and rest my head against the white ceramic tub and curl up. I want to cry, but I can't. So I close my eyes and let the water pour down over me.

chapter 13

I'm awake before the sunlight, my worried dreams interrupted by car alarms and distant sirens all night. My mother's sitting up, with her back to me. She hasn't slept, tells me it's because I was grinding my teeth in my sleep again.

Wozels is going into surgery to have a cancerous tumor removed from her gallbladder. We dropped her off yesterday morning, and when I asked the vet if she'd be all right, she looked at me with sorry eyes and told me again that Wozels is a very old dog. And then, with her hand on my shoulder, she said, "We'll do what we can, sweetheart."

We arrive at the clinic just after 9:30 a.m. The waiting room smells like kitty litter. A sloppy-jawed bulldog sleeps on the tile. There's a cat in a carrier. I sit with red eyes and bless myself again and again, clenching my fingers together until I'm white-knuckled, and pray.

The door opens, and a woman in blue scrubs steps out, a leash in her hands, and coaxes Wozels out of the back room. I see her white fur, and my eyes are hot and my vision blurs with tears. She's shaky-legged, disoriented, but she's alive. I kneel down and touch her, scoot closer and encircle her, rest my head against hers. Something's not right. The vet walks down the hall and smiles and tells us she's a strong little dog. The surgery cost sixteen hundred dollars and they'll send us a bill we'll never pay.

We drive back to the motel, Wozels facing me on my lap, a drugged look on her face.

We get her up the stairs, and she walks as if her legs might crumble into dust. I stand behind her and watch her struggle. She walks into the bathroom and lies down on the cool tile.

She doesn't eat her food that night. And as the months pass, she becomes weaker. Thinner. Frailer. Disappearing in front of me. Her rib cage protrudes through her soft fur. Her face is gaunt and sickly. She seldom stands, and when she does she walks into walls. I hold a plastic cup of water in front of her and force her to drink. She's sick for most of my senior year, and every day I walk home from class to the studio apartment my mother found for us and lie beside her on the bathroom floor under the fluorescent light. When we call the vet, she says there's nothing she can do, but she gives us pills that might improve Wozels's appetite. I spend my nights on the bathroom floor, wrapping her pills in bologna and trying to trick her into swallowing them. And every time, she spits the pill back out at me. No bologna to be found. And I smile and tell her she's just a puppy. I tell her she's my best friend. She sticks out her cold little tongue and licks my hand. And in my smallest voice, I ask her to hold on just a little while longer.

When she closes her eyes to sleep, I slip out and walk beneath piss-colored streetlamps with my head down, past closed tire shops and check-cashing stores. I sip chocolate milk at Denny's, alone in a semicircular corner booth big enough for a family of six, and write in my notebook.

A sunbaked East Mesa street lined with khaki-colored adobe homes and lawns of patchy dead grass. Brian and I wobble on his Go-Ped in broad, reckless arcs. I hold on to his waist, and he drives. He revs the engine, and we floor it up onto the sidewalk and hop off.

I run-step off the board and jog beside him as he idles and loops. We talk about graduating in a few weeks. How fast it all came. I've changed schools three times since starting high school—down to Florida and back, changing addresses—but we'll be graduating together. He says there's a big party planned after the ceremony and tells me I should come. He asks me about Wozels, and I lie and tell him she's okay.

"Isn't she really old?" he asks, and I say no, she's not so old. I change the subject, ask him about his new friends, the older junkie kids he's been going to lunch with. And he shrugs and tells me they're cool.

"Since when do you smoke weed?" I ask him. He says he only does it occasionally.

We arrive at his friend's house, a stucco-sided low-income town house. We go through the back gate and into the backyard, where two guys in their early twenties, Jesse and TJ, are repairing a bike with their shirts off.

We waste the day away.

I stay quiet and listen to them talk and smoke while heavy metal plays on the stereo. Stare up at the sky as it becomes infused with the navy-blue hue of night. Cans of warm Coors are everywhere, and ashtrays fill up with shriveled cigarette butts. Laughing and talking shit. Brian's cell phone rings, and his father asks him where he is, yells at him to come home. We can hear his voice through the phone.

He hangs up.

"You gotta go?"

He shakes his head. *Fuck it*, he says.

One of the older boys asks me to run inside to grab his lighter, and I do. I push the sliding glass door open and look around for it.

There's a bottle of vodka standing upright on the table. And I stare at it too long. I step closer. I know that label. I know the seductive, womanly shape of the bottle, the same one my mother picks up from the bottom shelf at the grocery store. I've seen it in my closet on Easter morning. Under the sink. Hidden beneath garage tarps puddled with wet leaves and old rain. It stares back at me, grins at me with charming eyes, gestures for me to come closer. It knows me. It's seen more of my family die than I have. It's always been here.

I can hear my friends laughing through the screen door, drunkenly telling stories. I walk closer to the bottle and pick it up, look closely at the label.

I wonder what it tastes like, what it feels like. I wonder if I can forget that Wozels is dying, if I can drink myself into another life the way the rest of my family did. I want to know what it feels like. I have to know what they did it for, what they gave it all away for.

I go outside with the bottle in my hand. I set it down, and they all look at me and laugh. They ask me what the fuck I'm going to do with the bottle.

I tell them I want to try it.

Dude, I thought you didn't drink, they all say, and I say,

I don't, then I unscrew the bottle top, lift it, press the warm plastic nozzle to my lips, close my eyes, and take a swig. Vodka floods into my mouth, feels like a thousand cactus needles in my sternum. Heat swells from beneath my tear ducts. I keep chugging. I can hear them cheering me on.

Fuck, yeah. Drink that shit, dude.

I'm gulping it now, the bottle emptying like an hourglass. Swig it again. Make a twisted, bitter face and do it another time.

I wipe my mouth and gasp. Drink some tepid water out of a Solo cup. Wipe my mouth. Take another swig.

My skin is warm. There's a fire crackling in my chest. A dizziness sets in. My eyelids are heavy. I look around the table.

He's fucked up, one of them says. *Look at him.*

I give him the finger, and they all laugh.

The smell of weed hovers around us. I put my head down, and I can see spinning blackness.

What the fuck is this?

The backyard is spinning.

Make it stop.

Life slips by like old slides through a projector. I'm standing by the edge of the pool. Cigarette smoke and chlorine in my nose. My face feels heavy. This is it.

And then I'm on my knees on white tile, screaming into the toilet bowl, and a volcano rush of water and vodka and chunky vomit spews into it. My head hangs into the ceramic bowl, which is cool on my cheek and temple, and I'm happy for a moment.

He's fucking puking, dude, one of them yells.

A dizzy spiral. I can smell the bitter toxins from my vomit.

My stomach roils like stormy waves. It's coming again. I gag and try to fight it.

Yell into the toilet bowl and vomit again.

I taste bad breath and stomach acid. Wipe my mouth.

I lie back on the tile. It's cold on my back.

I wake in the tub from fractured dreams.

My father as a young man sitting next to me in the backseat of a car. My mother as a little girl in the passenger seat, the same round face I'd seen a hundred times in yellowed photographs with the same short bob and freckles and missing front teeth. We're driving on the Long Island Expressway, approaching an underwater tunnel. My mother's on her knees in the passenger seat, turned around and facing me in the backseat. She tells me that when she was a little girl she used to be scared of going under water. She says she would drive with her father, and when they would approach the tunnel, she would hold her breath, her cheeks puffed out and her eyes wide, and she'd hold her breath until they drove through to the other end. Our car is eclipsed by the shadows and dark of the tunnel. And before we go through it, we hold our breath together. And through the window, I watch the shadows of sweet dolphins swim and somersault beside us, all along the tunnel's walls.

I wake up in a bedroom, sitting propped against a bed. The bubbling sounds of a bong hit. Porno on the TV. Some girl's getting fucked by a mechanic, screaming and moaning. Another fit of puking hits me, this time onto my shirt, my pants, vomit rolling out of my mouth.

Everyone groans. *Dude, what the fuck? Get him out of here.*

They grab me by my feet and drag me out of the room. The rug scrapes my lower back as they pull me through the living room. One of them opens the front door, and they drag me outside and onto the lawn.

Fuckin' idiot, one of them yells. And then he kicks me in the ribs, and I squeal. They laugh, and somebody kicks me again. I look around for Brian, but all I see are shoes and grass and a neighboring driveway. I lay my head down in the grass. I can feel something small and harmless crawling on my neck. I hear a drizzling sound. Smell piss. Laughter erupts. Jesse is pissing on me. I don't move. Just lie still on my back.

Soon I'm alone. Above me, miles of clear black sky dotted with white stars. The sky is spinning.

I wake up on the front lawn, the sun pressing against my face. Birds chirping. The neighbor's sprinkler is on. I'm not drunk anymore. I lift my head and look down at my clothes. I'm covered in puke and piss and grass strains. I feel dried vomit on my face. My shoulders are sore. My ribs hurt, but I can't remember why. I slowly get up. My body aches. I stand up and look to my right. An old man mowing his lawn waves at me. I smile and wave back. I go inside the house, which smells like cigarettes and weed. Jesse's asleep in the living room with the TV still on. I find my sneakers in the bathroom. I peel off my shirt and take off my jeans. I grab a towel and put it around my waist. In the bedroom, Jesse and TJ are asleep. The digital clock in the corner says it's just after 6:00 a.m. I go back outside wearing only a towel and some plaid boxer shorts and tube socks and sneakers, my puked-on clothes balled up in my hands.

It's too hot to be this early. I walk a mile to the next corner and check the street sign. I'm just a few miles from home.

I stick to the side of the road, but the roads are mostly

empty. I cut through a field and behind a strip of convenience stores and a Payless and an Applebee's. Up the road and back west, in the direction of the motel. I cut through a parking lot and run up the cement steps to our room and bang on the door twice.

My mother opens the door and looks me over.

"Where the fuck were you?"

"I was with Brian," I say.

She looks me in the eye. There's concern on her face. And then anger.

"Why are you in a goddamn towel? How'd you get home?"

I tell her I was at a party, and some guy threw up on me. She repeats my story back to me in a tone that says she knows I'm full of shit. And then she touches my face and looks at my eyes.

"You look like a ghost," she says. "What were you doing?"

"Nothing," I say, and I slip past her to check on Wozels. She's asleep on the bathroom floor, and when I turn on the light and the loud, broken fan, she groggily lifts up her head.

My mother stands in the doorway.

"So were you drinking?" she asks me.

I keep my face turned toward Wozels.

"No," I say. "I wasn't drinking."

She tells me to stand up and look her in the eye, and I do. She touches my cheek.

"You better not let me ever find you doing that shit," she says. "You understand me, Kenneth?"

I clench my jaw and fight the rush of tears that want so badly to rain down my face.

"Yes, I understand," I tell her.

*   *   *

Graduation day starts with an early morning dress rehearsal followed by a final day of classes tinged with unspoken melancholy. At sunset, the football field is flooded with hundreds of teenagers in blue caps and gowns and parents on their tiptoes snapping photos from the bleachers and girls crying and hugging and promising to stay in touch. I walk through crowds of seniors looking for my mother. I hear her piercing whistle and hug her. She takes a photo of us with a disposable camera, and she wants to see my diploma. Tells me she's proud of me.

Brian and the rest of our friends swarm around us.

"Hi, Mrs. New York!" they shout. They're older now, with wispy mustaches and deep voices. And my mother tells them all she's proud of them.

"You going to come party with us?" they ask her, and she laughs and says no, she's too old, but she wants us to go and have fun.

I hug her again and hand her my diploma and my cap and gown and run through the parking lot to catch up with Brian. I lift myself into the back of a pickup truck, and we peel out of the school together and down the road, hollering, with warm air blowing around us.

The house party spills out onto the front yard. There are four different schools' worth of graduating seniors at this stranger's house.

By 1:00 a.m. the party's dying down. I ask if anyone's seen Brian. Someone says she thinks he left and went to another party. My friend Heather says she's leaving soon if I need a ride. I check the bedrooms for Brian. The back bedroom is locked, and when I knock, a strange voice asks me who it is, then the door cracks open and a kid with sunken eyes and cherry-red swaths of acne asks me who the fuck I am. I peek behind him and see Brian asleep on the couch.

The room is shrouded in a gray veil of cigarette smoke. The spicy smell of incense wafts through thick air. Brian's head is back, his mouth open.

I step into the room slowly. Close the door behind me.

"I'm not used to you drinking yet, getting fucked up and all that," I tell him.

He kind of mumbles and wipes his mouth and readjusts his position on the couch. "You're a really special person," I continue timidly, my knee shaking. "And if you ever need anything, you can always ask me, and I'll be there."

My friend Heather pokes her head into the room.

"Kenny? We're leaving if you want a ride."

"I'll be right there," I answer.

She looks at me and at him and closes the door.

I stare at his face, pale and angelic, unblemished, brushed with freckles. I stand up and move toward the door. I look back at him, but he hasn't moved. I tell him to please be careful, then I turn the light out and leave.

chapter 14

It's morning. I stare at my guitar leaning against the wall in the corner of the room. Wozels is lying beside it with her eyes closed and the tip of her pale tongue peeking out of her mouth. I know she's dead, and so I turn around and walk to the other side of the room and rest my head against the wall and close my eyes.

She looks peaceful when I turn back to look at her, and there's a gentle morning light pressing through our dirty motel window that warms her. I kneel down beside her still body. I pet her fur, which feels different. I kiss her on her head and say, "I'm so sorry." I don't cry. I've been preparing myself for this moment since I first met her. I always knew the unfair impermanence of her friendship. And when I thought of her dying, when I'd imagine it on those days I'd walk home from school and kick rocks into the canal, it always involved me crying. But I'm not crying. I'm just staring at her. I think of all those kids who'd laugh at me when I'd wear my Wozels T-shirt to school, the ones who thought I was silly to love a dog so much, and I wonder for a moment if they had been right all along.

My mother stirs awake and looks over at me and she can tell by the look on my face that Wozels is gone. She says, "Baby girl?" and I nod as her eyes well with tears and she says, "Oh, my sweet girl, I'm so sorry," and hugs me and cries on my shoulder.

"She loved you so much!" she says into my T-shirt, and I tell her I know.

She rushes into the bathroom and shuts the old door and turns on the light and the faucet and the loud, dusty fan so she can cry alone. And I can hear her whimper through the door, over the running water, over the rusty vents.

When she comes out of the bathroom, I ask her what we should do, and she says she'll call animal control to pick her up. I sit down and rest the back of my head against the bed frame and look at Wozels's still body. This is a different kind of death from the kind I'm used to. I remember those earliest days, the two of us together in my bedroom, hidden away from all the yelling on the other side of the walls, and I'd stare at her, watching her head tilt and her ears perk, convinced she'd speak if I could just stay quiet long enough.

"Yeah, hello, my dog is—" my mother says. Her voice changes registers. "She died this morning, and I was wondering if I could have her body picked up by somebody, please."

The woman on the other end tells her to leave Wozels on the sidewalk, and they'll come pick her up.

"Leave her on the sidewalk? That's my baby, you mother-fucker!"

She slams down the phone.

"You hear this bitch on the other end? Leave her on

the sidewalk? How about I leave you on the sidewalk, you fuck!"

I tell my mother that I'll bury Wozels instead. We have a shovel in the storage unit. She wraps Wozels in a sheet and picks her up, and we walk together out into the hot morning and into the car. I say good-bye to my mother and drive Wozels down the side roads alone, looking in the rearview mirror at a lumpy sheet with a fluffy tail sticking out. I turn into the storage facility and park. I kneel down to open the padlock, and the loud metal door goes thwacking upward with a crash. There before me are the remnants of our most recent life. Familiar couches and boxes and bags of old toys and videotapes of TV shows and lamps and schoolbags full of our spelling tests and report cards. The shovel is way in the back, tucked behind a dresser and a bed frame. I climb over mountains of boxes, take it, and climb back out, grabbing the sliding roll-down metal door and forcing it down to the ground before locking it again.

I drive to our old block, which leads to the canal where I walked Wozels every day for so many years. I pick her up out of the backseat, cradle her head, and hoist her onto my shoulder. With my other hand I grab the shovel and set off down the canal to a cool, shadowed space shrouded in trees. I stomp on the ground. The dirt is a little softer here. I set Wozels down gently and take a deep breath. I pick up the shovel and start digging. I dig about three feet and pause. I'm sweating, and my palms are red and slightly calloused from the rough wooden handle. There is something wrong about this grave site. I imagine her out here alone at night, so far from me, pelted by rain, eaten by bugs.

"You don't want to stay here, do you?" I ask her. "You want to come home with me?"

I'm not ready. Maybe I can get her stuffed so I can keep her with me at all times. I imagine driving around with a stuffed Wozels sitting in my backseat. Waking up and seeing her sitting in the corner, motionless but still with me.

I grab the shovel and tuck it under my arm, bend down and hoist her up. I shuffle down the small dirt hill and get back into the car, where the heat is suffocating. The steering wheel is too hot to touch. I wrap it in newspaper, back out of the parking lot, and drive down the block.

"I'm sorry, Wozels," I say. "I'm trying."

I drive back to our neighborhood, then all the way to Wozels's vet. I open the door to a jingle. It smells clean, like Lysol. A bright-eyed woman welcomes me.

"Hot enough for you?" she asks.

I wipe my forehead.

"What can I do for you?"

I tell her my puppy passed away this morning, and she makes an exaggerated frown and tilts her head and tells me she's so sorry. I ask her about cremating options, and she hands me a pamphlet with some information, runs through some prices with me. It's not too expensive.

I imagine Wozels in a grand gold urn on my mantel, overlooking the dining room in the house I'll have someday, or in the passenger seat of the car as we go on road trips. Or I could sprinkle her ashes in some of the places she liked to go on her walks.

The woman tells me some people keep some of the ashes in a necklace, and I like that idea. I borrow her phone and call our motel room.

My mother answers.

I tell her I can't bury her. I'm going to have her cremated instead.

"Aww, poor baby girl," she says. I can tell she's crying again. She doesn't speak.

I hand Wozels to the woman and kiss my puppy one last time on the head. She tells me the procedure will take a few hours, and I sit in the air-conditioned waiting room, flipping through *Cosmo*. I take a quiz to see whether I'm an attentive lover.

Two swinging doors open down the hallway, and one of the veterinary assistants walks toward me holding a small white plastic rectangle just bigger than an eyeglasses case.

"Okay," she says. "We're all finished." I take the box from her. There's something heartbreaking about its lightness, something so undignified about the plastic container. I suddenly want to change my mind and leave her ashes behind and run out of the clinic.

"This is it?" I ask. "Are you sure?"

She nods and asks me if I was expecting it to be heavier. I don't know what I was expecting.

In the mornings, I walk to the local community college and attend a few classes, but I mostly daydream through them. Days blur into months. I spend my free time on the library computers using the Internet, mostly to read Roger Ebert's movie reviews. I spend hours making lists of his star ratings. I wish I knew how to write like he does, and when I try to write stories, I copy his style, borrow a few of his best lines, pretend his words are mine. I read his old reviews. I like the ones where he talks about loss, and I write down certain passages and take them as advice.

I am ashamed to admit that I feel relieved that Wozels is dead, but I do. I Google things like, "Is it normal to feel relief when your best friend dies?" and instead I find a support forum for mothers who've lost their children in Iraq, so I close the browser window. We've changed motel rooms since Wozels died, moved farther east to a motor lodge across from a dirt lot and up the road from a Kmart and a Wendy's.

I am quieter than usual. My mother asks me now and then if I want to go to the movies, and I say no. She says she's worried about me. I tell her I'm fine. I spend my time at the library, writing stories, maybe something about Wozels that might make me feel better, write a paragraph and erase it. I'm too embarrassed to let anyone read it, anyway. She was just a dog, and I'm afraid of what they'll say, afraid they'll laugh at me, not understand who she was. So I stare at the blank computer screen and wait for my free hour of Internet to expire.

I walk over to Brian's house and find him sitting on the curb fixing an old bike.

He nods to me. "You look like shit."

I tell him about Wozels, and he says, "Oh, Kenny, I'm so sorry."

He doesn't usually call me by my name, usually saying "dude" or some nickname. I sit down beside him. His skin looks different, and he's skinnier. He's started hanging around with guys I don't know, guys who were always a few years ahead of us in school. Junkie kids.

"You still taking classes at community?" I ask him, and he shakes his head.

"Nah, I stopped going a few weeks ago."

"What's up with you lately?" I ask him.

"What?"

"I don't know," I say. "I mean, you start hanging around a bunch of burnouts and now you're dropping out."

"And?"

"And nothing," I say. "You're just—"

"I'm what?"

"Different."

"How am I different?"

"I heard a story you were snorting up crushed pills at some party . . . doing coke and shit all of a sudden."

"I don't *do* coke," he says. "I *did* coke a few times, but I don't *do* coke. Don't be so fucking ignorant."

I tell him I'm thinking about moving up to Flagstaff, but I promise him we'll hang out when I come down to visit. We do our handshake. I tell him I'll see him soon.

The Greyhound bus pulls into the lonely Flagstaff station just after dark.

It's a small college town of snow-dusted streets with a downtown full of noisy pubs and a small improv theater and an occasional fast-food chain. Streetlights hang heavy on old wires. The main drag has a Target with a red neon sign and a Chili's and a Carl's Jr. and a Chase bank and a massive video-rental store. Farther down are abandoned factories. I cross the rusted train tracks with a backpack slung over my shoulder, shuffle down the hills past porch steps piled with dirty snow where the sun couldn't reach.

I haven't seen my brother in a few years. He calls now and then, but he usually pisses off my mother, then hangs up. I know that he's joined a fraternity. Kappa Alpha Order. Epsilon

Omega chapter. Lives in a big house he rents with friends I've never met.

It's getting dark as I walk the back roads to the Sizzler where my brother and his friends all work. Nighttime is different this far north. I wind down the roads and see the Sizzler sign across the street from the Denny's. I walk in, and it's warm and loud with conversation and smells like fried food. I see my brother in a black apron, taking the order of a large Navajo family at a table. He sees me and waves me over.

"I see you're still going with the gay homeless boy-band look," he says and hugs me.

"Come sit over here," he says and leads me to a raucous table of his friends, scruffy frat boys in T-shirts and flip-flops and backwards hats. Everyone says hi. A few give me stiff, vise-grip handshakes.

They say they've heard a lot about me, and I smile. One of them says he's sorry to hear about my dog, and I nod.

"Yeah, sorry," my brother says. "Mommy called me drunk saying you got her cremated and it's fuckin' creepy and she feels like it's staring at her at night and then she started screaming about Daddy and hung up."

"I have her with me. Wozels. She's in my backpack. Wanna see?"

I unzip my backpack and set Wozels on the Sizzler table.

"That's terrifying," he says, and I say I know.

He asks me if I'm okay, and I nod. I tell him I feel guilty for feeling relieved, for not crying.

"That's what you do," he says. "You feel guilty about stuff. That's kinda your thing."

He asks me if I've cried at all, and I say no.

"Maybe it hasn't sunk in quite yet," he says, and I nod.

* * *

I rent a small room from one of my brother's friends for about two hundred dollars a month. It's unfurnished, but I make a bed out of heavy blankets and quilts and sleep on the floor next to Wozels's ashes. I'm fired from a job at the Sizzler and another at a Chinese restaurant, but I finally get a job at Home Depot and buy my first cell phone, a cheap flip phone I use to call my mother. She's moved into her mother's back bedroom. She tells me she started crying at the grocery store when she walked down the dog-food aisle out of habit. And she still can't find the goddamn remote. She thinks one of the Mexican movers stole it.

The people at Home Depot are nice to me, but I'm not so good at the job. I don't know anything about tools or screws or wood and my money drawer is always unbalanced and I receive a verbal warning after failing a secret-shopper test. My shifts begin at 7:00 a.m., and I sit in my car, a piece-of-shit 1989 Eagle Premier I bought for three hundred dollars, in the empty Home Depot parking lot eating an Egg McMuffin and hash browns. My knuckles are red. No heater. I blow hot air into my hands. Rub them together. Hide my fingers under my arms.

After work I walk to the campus library and use my brother's log-in and password to read Ebert's reviews. I write stories and mimic his style. Daydream. I'm lonely here.

I hear through a friend of a friend that Brian's using heroin, that he started just after I left for Flagstaff. He started snorting it at first, and then, once he got over his fear of needles, he began shooting it into the veins in his arms, and when the mustard-stain bruises became too noticeable, he started shooting it between his toes.

*   *   *

On my days off I wander through the mall on the other side of town. Window-shop. Page through books in the small bookstore. A kiosk selling gold necklaces has a holiday special, and I see a small gold chain with a dog-bone-shaped piece of fake gold on the end. I buy it and have them engrave Wozels's name on it, and I wear it around my neck. On the fifteenth of the month, I get my check and cash it and go to the movies alone. At night I walk alone to the corner store for a snack, then wander the streets. Past the motor lodges, the check-cashing stores, the bare trees and black woodland. An occasional coyote peeks his head out of the darkness, then scatters. Stretches of dark road, miles of nothingness, then a Walmart.

I pack a small bag and buy a bus ticket down to Mesa to visit my mother for the weekend. The bus struggles down steep cliffs, winds around roads carved into the sides of towering mountains. The Mesa bus terminal is near our old motel, and my mother picks me up and takes me to my grandmother's house in the retirement community. The house smells like Sea Breeze astringent. *Charlie Rose* is playing on a small TV.

My grandmother is happy to see me. She's still bald and still wearing a surgeon's mask over her face. With her hand over her mouth, she tells me the Italian man next door is poisoning her dog. She thinks he's in the Mafia.

"All right, enough, Mother!" my mother says. My mother asks me if I can go to the storage space to look for the goddamn remote so she doesn't have to watch CNN all day. I drive her car through town and to the unit, where our furniture is in the same arrangement as we left it. I don't know where to begin, so I start ripping the brown duct tape from the boxes. Forks and knives. No remote. Another box. School papers. Another box. Wrestling toys. Batman toys. I climb over the dresser and check between the mattresses. It could be anywhere. Check in the dresser drawers. No remote. I pull the cushions off the couch and feel around in the creases. No remote. I feel something else. My heart sinks. I pull one of Wozels's old doggy biscuits from the depths of the couch. She must have hidden it there. I think about the way I used to ask her to dance before I'd give her one. And how she'd rise up on her hind legs and perk up those ears and wave her paws at me. And when I'd give it to her, she'd want to run outside with it. Bury it for later. A warm tear falls out of my eye and onto my wrist. Another onto the concrete floor. I sit on the edge of the cushionless couch, elbows on my knees, tears running down my face. And then I sink to the concrete floor and scream into my hands.

Scream until my face is heavy with blood and dry spit hangs out of my mouth and the veins bulge in my neck. I scream into this echoless storage unit. I scream until my throat is raw and shredded.

And finally, I cry, and cry, and cry.

chapter 15

It seems to always be winter in Flagstaff. Work is the same. It's been six months, and I'm training to work in the garden department. My boss tells me that maybe one day I'll be a shift leader. Every month or so I sit in a back storage room and watch a training video in which a cartoon hammer talks about sexual harassment in the workplace.

After work I go for walks through acres of bare, hostile forest that somehow survived another year of bitter cold. I'm not so good at making friends. I don't get to see my brother as much as I thought I would. He has a whole other life here that's all his own, a new girlfriend he spends most of his time with. I go to the movies alone, bringing in my own cup of coffee, because that's what Ebert does. And afterward I wander the quiet streets. Not sure how I got here. Sometimes I talk to Wozels the way I used to, pretend she's still with me.

I think about failure a lot lately. Staring out of city bus windows at the passing streetlights. Scanning bar codes. Making chitchat with customers. I think about it. I'm afraid it's in my blood. And time's going by so quickly now. Some-where between the motel rooms and minimum-wage jobs, between sleep and sitcoms, switching schools and dying rel-atives, I became an adult. But I don't feel like much of one. I just feel lost in this city, carrying my dog's ashes around with me, talking to ghosts, and working jobs that make my small dreams feel like the punch line to a very long joke.

The patrons of the Flagstaff public library are mostly retired women and homeless men. After my shift at Home Depot ends, I spend my days here writing stories. After I get out a single paragraph I feel exhausted. Exhausted. Erase it, say *Fuck it*, log off, and storm out. I wander the hallways of the university, which looks like a nice school. I applied when I first arrived, but didn't get in. There was a problem with my high school transcripts. During my time in Florida I had missed too many days and lost credit for an entire year. When I returned I attended a charter school for juvenile delinquents, but the registrar of the university told me the school was unaccredited and my grades there won't be recognized. I peek inside class-rooms. Read the fliers on the walls for internships, job open-ings. I overhear two kids talking about the internships they've gotten. One kid is going to Connecticut to intern at ESPN. The other is going to Radio Disney.

For extra money, I drive the three hours south to Phoenix on the weekends and work with my mother at the Arizona State Fair, where Ferris wheels are set up in the parking lot of a Kohl's department store that used to be a Mervyn's. My mother works behind an outdoor cash register wearing a plastic hairnet and a bright yellow polo shirt that says PIGGLY WIGGLY on it. Piggly Wiggly sells chili fries and deep-fried onion rings and fried zucchini and large ground-beef drumsticks.

I'm wearing a hairnet and working in the fryer today, a narrow trailer packed with line cooks sweating over boiling oil alongside metal crates full of onions and potatoes that get fried and dried and served through the small slots in the windows. It's mostly ex-cons in here. The guy to my left is named Cowboy. He did ten years for robbery. Still has the lost years in his eyes. He has a gentle way about him. Cowboy shows me how to load the fryer full of cut potatoes. Tells me to watch out for the boiling oil. Shows me a scar he got from it. My mother yells in orders from outside. She's sweating. It's 110 degrees out. We're suffocating in here. The orders never end. The oil bubbles.

I see my mother, who's eating a burger and sitting on a bench.

"Hot enough for you? Jesus Christ," she says.

I sit down next to her.

"You meet Cowboy? You know he robbed a bank?"

"You told me."

"Well, stay away from him. You don't need to be getting buddy-buddy with him. They'll find you in the canal with a knife in you."

"That's nice," I say.

"I'm serious," she says. "I don't trust any of these motherfuckers. I'm just here for a paycheck. Shoulda heard him the other day. Saying all kinds of disgusting shit to me, to the other women here. Real pig mouth. Just be careful," she says.

Cowboy's sitting on the small stepladder that leads up to the fry trailer, smoking a cigarette.

"Your mom tells me you're a writer," he says. "What do you write?"

I tell him I don't really know. Stories.

"Yeah, I got a story for you," he says. He smiles, revealing missing teeth. "I got stories that'd keep you up at night. I've seen some crazy shit."

He says his life is a lot different now, calmer. Boring. Sucks on his cigarette.

He asks me what I'm doing here, and I tell him I'm trying to earn some extra money. He asks me if I'm in school, and I say no. Asks me how old I am, and I say I'm eighteen. He says he wishes he were eighteen again. Wishes he had gone to school. He wishes he could do a lot of things over again.

He asks me to take his phone number, call him sometime so he can tell me his story. I scribble it down on a napkin.

"Not sure if this phone is still gonna be good after this week, but you'll find a way to get hold of me," he says.

I drive back up to Flagstaff for my Sunday morning shift at Home Depot. When I arrive the shift leader tells me to go into the back office to see my boss, who asks me where I was Friday night. I tell him I was working a second job down in Phoenix.

"A second job? You had a shift here Friday," he says. "One to nine. You forget?"

He points to the schedule on his desk.

I tell him I'm sorry. I had forgotten. It won't happen again.

He says he's sorry, too, but they're going to have to let me go.

I drive myself back down to Phoenix. My mother has a friend who has a friend who has a job collecting signatures on street corners for an education petition the city is trying to pass. She says they'll pay me two dollars per signature.

I stop strangers and passersby.

"Hi…would you mind signing a petition for the education…"

They wave me off, keep walking.

It's so fucking hot.

I have eight signatures. I do the math in my head. Sixteen bucks. I find some shade to hide under until people walk by, then I run out and approach them.

"Hi…would you mind signing a petition…"

They keep walking.

I take the bus across the city to Tempe, the college town where Arizona State University is based. There's a long stretch of bars and clubs and restaurants that surround the school, and I have better luck here. Six more signatures.

A shirtless white guy with Rasta dreads walks his bike across the crosswalk and approaches me to tell me he'll sign. I thank him and ask him if he's an Arizona resident, and he says yes. Says he has a felony.

"They won't accept it if you have a felony," I say.

"Sorry, bro."

I ask him what the felony is for, and he says he's been arrested for drugs, fighting, domestic violence, and robbery.

"Pretty much everything but sex with a minor," he says, laughing. "But I still got time!"

He asks me where I'm from. "Why you doin' this shit? I got some friends who do this shit, but they're felons. Can't do anything else."

I tell him I needed a job in a hurry.

He sits and lights a joint, tells me to keep an eye out for police. Asks me if I've ever snorted bath salts. I say no, and he tells me a story about a weekend he spent high on them in New Mexico that ended when he tried to fork out his own eye.

"I'll be right back," I tell him.

I cross the street and go through the campus and into the main ASU building, a brand-new structure, all glass and marble.

It's cool inside. I slurp tepid water out of the water fountain. Wander the hallways, where I see bulletin boards covered with fliers for internships, just like the bulletin boards in Flagstaff. I peek inside classrooms. I grab some fliers off the walls, the ones advertising journalism internships, and plug the thumbtacks back in. Fold up the fliers and put them in my back pocket. Walk through a café and into a large, mostly empty library. I sit down at a computer and exhale. I pull some of the fliers out of my pocket and e-mail the editors of newspapers and magazines, asking them for an internship. I don't know how to write a cover letter or a résumé. I just tell them who I am and that I'll work for free. Weeks go by, and I wait to hear from them. Most of them don't respond, but the few who do ask me if I'm a college student. When I say no, they tell me they're sorry, but they can't help. The internships go to students from accredited universities.

I walk back out into the oppressive sunshine. The Rasta-dread homeless junkie calls me over. He's set himself at a table in the corner by a Starbucks with his bike, his bags, all the trinkets he's accumulated. I walk over to him and sit down. He asks me if I want to make some real money. He pulls some beach stones out of a yarn pouch and places them on the table. He tells me the stones look like famous people, and he's going to become a millionaire.

This one is Sandra Bullock, he says, and pushes it toward me.

I don't see the resemblance.

"You help me sell these, and you'll be a millionaire in no time," he says.

He reminds me of my uncle Carter. Smiling, smoking, making promises. And I want to tell him I'm so sorry. I want to hug him and help him. But I know that vacant look in his eyes. And so I tell him no, it's not for me, and I get up and walk back to my corner and ask strangers for signatures until dusk arrives.

Sometimes I wonder what will become of me. I want to be a lot of things, but I'm too embarrassed to say any of it, so I keep it to myself. Sometimes it's to be a writer. But sometimes I change my mind. Maybe I'll be a movie director. Sometimes I want to be a rock star, and I play air guitar in my room until somebody knocks and barges in and I pretend I was doing push-ups. I keep a list of my favorite authors. A lot of them teach in colleges around the country, and I send them letters there, asking them if they need an assistant or an intern. When I wander around at night, scuffing my old shoes on the streets, I imagine one of them saying yes and taking me on to work with him in a small house together. Maybe a writer who feels forgotten and needs somebody to believe in him. But nobody writes me back.

On an otherwise slow weekday, back in Flagstaff, I read a new article on Roger Ebert's website. One of his favorite directors received an NC-17 rating for depicting graphic sexuality, and Ebert lambastes the Motion Picture Association of America for rating sex more harshly than violence. And right then and there I decide I want to make a documentary about the MPAA and their evil, puritan ways. I have no filmmaking skills, no money, no equipment, no experience, no guidance, and I own absolutely nothing, not even a real bed, but I want to meet Ebert, and I figure this is as good a way as any. I send a letter to the *Chicago Sun-Times*, the newspaper where he works, asking for his e-mail address. A few days later, an assistant responds and tells me to write a letter to Ebert's assistant, Monica Gelfund. And so I do. I tell her I'm a filmmaker making a documentary about the MPAA and ask her to forward my message to her boss. And then I imagine her reading my letter, rolling her eyes, and making a masturbatory gesture with her right hand before discarding it in a pile with the thousands of other letters they've received.

The next day I go straight to the public library and log on for my free hour of Internet. I check my Hotmail account. Junk mail. Some porn. Coupons for pizza.

And an e-mail from Roger Ebert.

I stare at his name in my in-box. It looks fake. I click on it before I can chicken out.

> Dear Mr. Porpora,
> I am very busy but it may be that my producer, Don DuPree, could set up a time when we could discuss your project. I'd like to hold it to 15 minutes.
>
> Best,
> Roger

I immediately close out of the screen. I get up from my chair and walk in circles like a dog chasing his tail. I sit back down.

I have fifty-six minutes of free Internet left. I log back in to my Hotmail. There's his name again. Roger Ebert. It seems so silly for me to have such an important person's name in my in-box. I wonder if he knows I'm eighteen and got fired from Home Depot and sleep on a pile of borrowed blankets. I wonder if he knows I have a giant teddy bear named Roger E-Bear that sleeps on my blanket bed next to Wozels's ashes.

Ebert has responded. And for the first time in my life I feel like I could actually make something of myself. And then I panic.

I'm in so far over my head. *What the fuck am I gonna do?!*

I call my brother.

"What's up, fag?"

"So ya know how I love Roger Ebert?"

"Mmm-hmm..."

"Well, I had this idea to make a documentary about the MPAA, and—"

"What the fuck is that?"

"Never mind. It's the people that rate movies, R, PG-13, whatever..."

"All right..."

"And I e-mailed Ebert and told him I'm a documentarian and that I'm making a movie about them, and he agreed to let me interview him!"

"You're a retard," he says. "What are you gonna do?"

"I don't know. I didn't think he'd respond. No one ever responds!"

"Who else have you e-mailed?"

"Everybody!" I say. "I just e-mail people sometimes. Ask for jobs, internships, whatever."

"Like who?"

"I dunno...fuckin' Al Gore, Bill Clinton, magazine editors..."

"Al Gore? What the fuck did you ask Al Gore for?"

"I dunno. I just tell them I want to get my foot in the door and ask if they need help. But everyone fucking ignores me. So I sent an e-mail to Roger Ebert on a whim."

"So now what?"

"I dunno. I need equipment and money, and I need to find a way to get to Chicago."

"One sec," he says, and I hear him repeating the story to his friends. The room explodes in laughter.

"Chris wants to know if you told Ebert about your teddy bear."

"No."

"Did you tell him you were recently fired from the Sizzler? Everyone thinks you're autistic. I have to go," he says and hangs up.

I look at Ebert's e-mail staring back at me. I e-mail him back, speaking out loud in a deep voice as I type, hoping to sound professional.

> Dear Mr. Ebert,
> Thank you for the prompt response. I can't tell you how excited I am to discuss my project further

I delete and start again.

> I can't tell you how excited my team and I are to discuss my project further. I will contact your producer and organize a time to meet.
> Thank you for your time.
>
> Best,
> Kenny

I've never used *Best* before, but Ebert used it, and so I will use it to close every e-mail I ever write for the rest of my life.

I'm going to fuck this up somehow. I'm pretty sure this is going to end with Ebert filing a restraining order. I call his producer, and he answers, pleasant and professional, and he tells me Ebert will be in Hawaii for a film festival, then back for TV tapings. He asks me what my schedule looks like, and because it looks like asking strangers for signatures and avoiding the homeless junkie with Rasta dreads and cooling off in a Carl's Jr. bathroom—I tell him I'm wide open. We pick a date. A Wednesday a few weeks from now. He says the staff can shoot the interview for me using the equipment in the *Ebert & Roeper* studios. It'll already be lit right and wired for sound, and that way my team won't have to lug all their equipment. I tell him in that case it'll just be me. Traveling alone.

I spend my final Home Depot paycheck on my flight to Chicago Midway. And for the next few weeks I do as much research on the MPAA as I can, take notes, write and rewrite questions. I come up with a list of ten questions, and I time myself asking them over and over in the mirror. I don't want to run past fifteen minutes. I pick out my best shirt to wear, and I pack a small bag. I set three alarms the night before my flight but still ask my mother to call me so I won't oversleep.

chapter 16

It's a different kind of cold in Chicago. Stinging, relentless. And the wind's like a bully, tearing at me, scratching my face like loose tree branches. I'm afraid I'll get lost if I venture too far out, so I stay near the motel, a Red Roof Inn next door to an Applebee's. I walk in circles around the block, my sweater pulled up over my mouth, my hands over my ears. My outfit for tomorrow is laid out on my mattress. I've called my mother. She reminded me to tell Ebert that I played the Joker in my living room when I was five, acted out scenes, directed my brother. She wants me to show him the stories I've written.

I arrive back at my room, which has heavy maroon drapes and a matching bedspread. It's after midnight, and I need to sleep, but I pace with the list of questions I typed and printed out before I came. Go over them in my head. Time myself again. I don't want anything to go wrong.

I'm scared awake by my courtesy wake-up call. I bury my head into the pillow, still tired. Five more minutes. And then I hear my mother's voice telling stories, the one about my uncle Carter and how he was always late. My grandfather, too. That's the Kruger way, she'd say with a laugh. I open my eyes and force myself out of bed and dress quickly. Go over the questions again. Time myself. Bless myself.

The wind begins its attack as soon as I walk out into the early morning air. It never stops its assault. I walk through the Loop, past rushing cabs and chugging buses, hurried businessmen in nice suits. I read my handwritten directions off the back of a receipt. A left and another left. And then the first right. I arrive at the studio, which is in a tall, impressive building that has a lobby of gold and marble.

I'm three hours early.

At the front desk, a jovial man greets me and asks whom I'm here to see.

"I'm here to see Roger Ebert," I tell him. It's the proudest moment of my whole life.

He asks me when my appointment is, and I tell him it's not until the afternoon. He gives me a visitor's sticker and says I can wait in the lobby or at the Potbelly Sandwich Shop next door.

I sit in the Potbelly and count the hours. I eat less than half my sandwich, and the soft roll hardens in front of me. When I accidentally spill a drop of ketchup on my list of questions, I have a quiet nervous breakdown in my seat.

It's just before one when I return to the lobby, and I wave at the guy at the front desk and go through the turnstile. I take the elevator alone up to some high-numbered floor. The gold elevator doors open, and I'm greeted by Don DuPree, Ebert's producer, who shakes my hand energetically and thanks me for coming. As we walk down the hallway making small talk, I think it's going okay, mostly because he hasn't yet told me that this whole thing is a big joke and that he's sending me home to fry zucchini in a trailer with an ex-con.

We turn the corner and walk onto a claustrophobic TV set. And I see Ebert, his cheeks rosy like a ceramic Santa's, wearing a sweater vest and his trademark eyeglasses, the *Ebert & Roeper* logo behind him. He sees me and smiles. I approach him and shake his hand and tell him how great it is to meet him. He's serious, but his smile is warm and his voice is grandfatherly, or at least what I imagine a grandfather's voice could be.

I tell him I'll be sure to keep it to fifteen minutes, and he says, "Take as much time as you need. I'm here for you." The production crew asks me if a medium shot is good, and I nod. Perfect. A medium shot. Whatever the fuck that is.

My hands are shaking and my knees are shaking and my voice is shaking. I read my questions directly off my sheet of paper, making occasional eye contact. I rattle off my first question—*You've discussed the MPAA's tendency to rate sexuality more harshly than they do violence. Can you talk a bit about why you think this is?*—and Ebert nails his answer. I nod along with everything he says. He's even better in person.

I ask my second question, and Ebert stumbles a bit, stops himself, gathers his thoughts, takes the editing process into consideration with a slight pause, then fires off another answer. I wish I were a better interviewer, but I just nod and smile and go down my list, keeping my hand over the ketchup stain.

Fifteen minutes later, it's over.

He asks me if I'm sure I got everything I need, and I say yes.

While the production crew gets the tape ready for me to take home, Don DuPree joins us on the small stage and says he thinks it went well.

"Me, too," I say. I build up some courage and ask Ebert if

he has an assistant or an intern, and he says I'd have to talk to Don about that—Don handles all the college internships. He asks me if I'm in college, and I say no. I'm not.

"You went to University of Illinois at Urbana-Champaign," I tell him.

"I did," he says.

He tells me one of his big regrets in life is that he was never a graduate student. I decide right there that I want to be a graduate student. He tells me there are lots of good schools in New York. Columbia's a great one, he says, and so Columbia it is.

And then he touches my arm and tells me there's another filmmaker making a documentary about the same subject.

I had a feeling.

He says the director is well known and has a lot of experience and is already pretty far along.

I thank him for letting me know and ask him what he thinks I should do.

He shrugs, and in a gentle voice, he says, "You just got to keep trying until you make it."

He asks me if I've thought about college. He tells me he thinks I'd be good at it. I tell him I'll look into it. The production team is ready with the tape, and it's time for me to go. I want to hug him and tell him how much I appreciate his keeping me company in all those lonely libraries. But instead I shake his hand and thank him again.

I wake up in Flagstaff.

Whatever hope I had after the meeting soon dulls to zombie-eyed self-loathing. The burden of daily life is heavier than a sound bite of encouragement from my idol. Days are lost to boredom and the Internet. I tell myself things even if they're lies. Promise myself I'm not lazy. I'm not like them. I don't have my uncle's eyes. Or my father's nose. Or their fucking blood. I won't get stuck in this shitty town. But I can still hear them at the dining table, every one of my dead relatives, laughing at those conformist chumps, those suckers, those assholes who went to college and work nine-to-five jobs, those dead-eyed slaves, those corporate suits, before laughing and loading up their bongs and pouring vodka over ice.

I replay Ebert's words in my head. Tell myself to keep going. I haven't read much of anything, and so I make lists of books you're supposed to read and find them on shelves with new book jackets and pick them up, page through them, and put them down. I sit in Dunkin' Donuts with John Updike and read the same page six times until I zone out because I'm a fucking idiot who's never been any good at school and I'll never be anything but a cashier at Home Depot in this fucking town. Force myself to sit back down and pick the book up again.

I close the book. *Goddamn it.*

Rest my head in my hands.

I'm not such a great reader. I never have been. And the dreams I've kept for so long to myself, the ones I lose myself in when I work my new job—the day shift at Red Lobster—are starting to do nothing but remind me how small I am. And time keeps barreling on. Birthdays arrive suddenly, unwelcome, like the end of summer. The community college up here tells me my high school credits won't be accepted by any college because most of the courses at the charter school weren't accredited. He says I'll need to take the GED.

And so I stack Faulkner and Hemingway and Bellow and

Cheever beside stacks of GED study guides. I feel like a fraud reading these books. I read and highlight and zone out. Read again. I feel like I'm too far behind.

On one otherwise forgettable midweek day, I pick up a book of poems edited by Garrison Keillor called *Good Poems for Hard Times*. I know Keillor's name from Ebert's essays, and I page through it looking for hope. But instead I find a poet named Stephen Dunn. And he speaks in plain language about loss and landscapes that sound so familiar to me and bring small tears to the corners of my eyes. He writes about his dead parents. His silence. His failed marriages and his enduring dreams. I look at his photo on the back of the book and see a bearded man who looks like he enjoys a good pipe, and I read in his bio that he studied at Hofstra University. On Long Island.

I haven't spoken to my father in six years, never knowing what kind of legal repercussions would come from calling him. My mother would tell us he'd drag us back to court, more cops, more moving. But I'm older now. And those days feel so long ago. I text my mother and ask her if she has my father's number.

My mother hasn't quite learned how to text:

242-9734 xOXO jETS lOSE! bOO! @! tHEY sUCK. 7&hAVE a GrooVY dAy! lOVE mOM & baby wOZEls!

I dial his number, and he picks up. His familiar voice answers. "Hello?"

"Dad?"

"Who's this? Stevie?" he asks excitedly.

"It's Kenny," I say.

"Ken!" he says with a great exhale of relief and joy. "How the hell are you, kiddo?"

He sounds the same. I thought it would feel strange to speak to him, but it doesn't. "I'm good," I say. "I'm up in Flagstaff with Steve."

"Flagstaff: Is that in Arizona?" he says.

"Yes," I say. "But it's way far north. It snows."

"Hang on, let me turn the TV off," he says, setting the phone down. I can hear *Everybody Loves Raymond* in the background.

"I was watching *Raymond*. Not bad. So what's up? It's been so goddamn long I don't even know where to begin," he says.

He starts to cry.

"You know, after your mother took you away again, I couldn't fight her anymore. I was just too goddamn old, you know?"

"I know," I say.

"I think about you and your brother every day."

He says he heard about Wozels, and he's sorry.

"That just broke my heart," he says, and he starts to cry again. He tells me he's been singing again. Nursing homes and libraries and assisted living centers. He's moved to the upstairs portion of our house. Found a tenant to rent the basement. Some Puerto Rican. He says he almost has enough money saved to buy the house back.

I tell him I think that's great.

"How's everybody else?" I ask.

He's quiet.

"They're all gone, kiddo. Uncle George, your aunt Marie,

Uncle Frank, Aunt Nancy, Uncle Danny, Auntie Alice, Uncle Bart..."

It's not like my mom's family. My father's side of the family died mostly from just getting old, but they're all gone now.

I take a deep breath. "Are you okay?"

"Yeah...when Georgie died I cried. That was a sad one. Remember how he used to buy those orange pops when you'd come to visit?"

I smile. Yes, I say.

"For a while there it seemed like there was a funeral every month."

My prepaid phone starts to beep. I'm running out of time.

I tell him I've been thinking about going to college. Found a poet I like a lot who studied at Hofstra, and I'm thinking of doing the same.

"Coming here?" he says. "Of course. I'd love to see you. You can come anytime. Stay as long as you'd like."

MacArthur Airport on Long Island is small, with just a few terminals. I walk past the Hudson News stand, down the escalator, and out of the building. The familiarity of Long Island crushes me. And then I see my father making his way through the parking lot, and I go toward him. I am taller than he is now. His hair is gray and thin, slicked back, and his neck skin is looser.

I bend down to hug him. "Holy shit, you got big!" he says. "Let me get your bags."

The drive home is awkward. His new car is twenty-six years old and rattles and smokes as we drive. He tells me about his new mechanic, some Mexican guy he found in the *Pennysaver* after Uncle Bob died. The streets outside the window are from my childhood. The names on the forest-green signs ring bells, like old friends I never wanted to see again.

We pull onto our block, and the old car stutters past the same houses I remember. The same aluminum siding.

The house is damp and smells faintly like mildew. The thin brown carpet is still there. An old TV sits on a desk cluttered with nuts and bolts and napkins and old newspapers and mustard-stained paper plates and screwdrivers and old mint tins full of thumbtacks. On the kitchen door frame, pencil marks measuring my height. My brother's height. The tallest mark comes up to my chest.

There's a school photo of me tacked to the wall. It must be twelve years old. I'm baby-faced, with puffed-out cheeks, shaggy hair, and dark circles under my eyes. And on the refrigerator door, a more recent photo of my father and me with our baseball gloves, smiling wide. I look on the back of the photograph, where my father has scribbled in blue pen: THE BABY AND DAD, 1995.

I walk down the hallway, past my father's fist holes covered with off-white plaster and masking tape, and push open the flimsy wooden door to the bedroom I slept in as a child. It's so small I almost feel like I need to duck to be inside. The same orange-and-yellow walls. The same alphabet stickers on the closet door. The same photographs of my mother and Wozels taped up for the nights when I couldn't kiss them good night.

That night we watch *Everybody Loves Raymond* in the dark and eat pasta while a box fan blows warm air onto us.

"Who's the tenant?"

"Some guy, Angel, Puerto Rican, forties, and his mother. She's this big!" he says, and gestures his hand, palm down, about three feet off the floor.

"She calls me Don Louie. She says, 'Don Louie, you take me to store?' And I say, 'Yeah, I'll take you to store.' And she comes back from the hairdresser and she says, 'Don Louie, guess how old?' And I lie and say, 'I dunno, fifty?' And she proudly says, 'Seventy-seven.' I wanna say, 'Yeah, you look a hundred and ninety.' And she brings me up weird food. Big platters covered in cellophane. I opened one once. Beans and corn stalks. I threw it away. But they pay the rent on time, and they're quiet. Never a problem."

We eat and watch TV. Forks scraping on plates.

"He's a goddamn drunk," he continues. "That black barrel outside? Full, every night. Beer cans. Liquor bottles. Holy shit. And..."

He waves me in close.

"They can hear everything," he whispers. "I think he's a little weird. He's got all kinds of children's toys down there. And I found these notebooks in the trash. Stories about young boys having sex together."

The light from the TV reflects off his face.

"So why don't you throw him out?" I ask.

"Oh, are you gonna pay me four hundred dollars a month? Because he pays the rent and I've had three tenants come and go and I need the money."

We go back to eating. Raymond's wife thinks they should go on a date to recapture the magic.

"You know who I'd love to get down there?" he says. "An old Chinese couple. She could cook for me. And he could teach me the Internet. But I can't go around posting fliers that say 'Looking for Chinese couple to live in my basement,' you know?"

"I can teach you the Internet," I tell him.

"I took a class over at the library. Some redhead was teaching the class, cute little thing, and she comes up to me talking a million miles a minute—take the mouse, go here, do this, click here, delete that, move this—I says, 'Whoa, whoa, whoa: What's the mouse?'"

I laugh at him.

"All right," he says. "I'm gonna hit the sack." He kisses me on the head. "I'm glad you're here," he says.

"I am, too," I say.

I look for work in Bay Shore, but my interview at Chili's doesn't go well. I've chosen a date to take the GED at some high school up the road, and I try to study in quiet library rooms, afraid I'm going to fail at this, too. On the morning of the test I'm up early, out the door before 7:00 a.m. Drive my father's clunker of a car past houses with ghosts in the aluminum siding, conjuring unwanted memories. I arrive at the school and sit at a long table in the empty cafeteria before it fills up with teen moms and dreadlocked white girls and black girls with fake nails and a guy in a tank top with one pant leg rolled up to show off his house arrest ankle bracelet.

I take the test quickly. Fill in the bubbles with my number 2 pencil. Keep my head down. Watch the clock and finish before 2:00 p.m. Turn it in. Six weeks later my father calls me to tell me that I passed.

The office of the dean of the School of University Studies at Hofstra has a small waiting room furnished with orange and yellow plastic chairs. I sit in one and flip through *Smithsonian* magazine, my knee softly shaking. The door opens, and a small woman who looks to be in her sixties emerges, holding my application in her hands.

Her name is Elizabeth. Inside her office, which is lined with bookshelves, I sit in the swivel chair beside her desk. She slips my personal essay out of a manila folder and reads through it again. My essay is a little about my life. How I got here. And a little bit about meeting Roger Ebert. I'm hoping she'll read some sort of ambition in my words. But my transcripts are a mess, spotty and unimpressive. I barely passed some of my high school classes.

She looks up at me from over her reading glasses.

"So why don't you start telling me a little bit about why you're here?" she says. There's a seriousness about her; it's clear she has no time for bullshit.

"Well," I say, "I want to be a graduate student."

She smirks a bit and tells me to slow down. "The thing is," she says, "your transcripts don't quite meet our standards. However, we offer this program for students we think have potential. You could think of it as acceptance for a probationary period. You'd take a full course load. I would teach your core class. And then it would be up to you. Either you'll meet our standards, and we'll allow you in full-time, or you won't." She tells me she's afraid the costs will be considerable and I'll need to take out a bank loan and apply for financial aid.

She asks me if I think I'm up to it, and I say yes.

"Try not to let me down," she says.

The night before my first day of school, I lie in the small bed in my childhood room and watch the clock. I worry the car won't start in the morning. Or there'll be traffic. Something will go wrong. It always does. And so I leave early and arrive early. Sit in the dark classroom and wait. Elizabeth arrives, and she smiles when she sees me sitting there. She gives us the syllabus, and I go to the bookstore and buy my books and sit in the Dunkin' Donuts across the street and read. I start early because I read slowly. And I read the same line again. And again.

I have a philosophy class in the evening. Ethics. I sit in the front row with my hoodie pulled over my head and listen. I don't look around me. I can't make friends. I'm too distractible, can't risk failing.

This is Stephen Dunn's old school, and so the library has all his old books, even the ones that are out of print. I take small breaks from my textbooks and read his poems in the stacks. The rest of the time I study. And write. Close my eyes to the doubt. Because this has to work.

chapter 17

On my days off I help my father with his nursing-home gigs, which means I spend a lot of time in dementia units.

We're celebrating a birthday today at a nursing home in the Catskills. Somebody's turned ninety. We break for birthday cake and lousy coffee. After the show I help my father pack up his equipment and wires while he helps the attendants wheel some of the patients back to their rooms.

Once we've loaded the equipment into the trunk, my father tries starting the car, and it stalls.

He revs it again. The engine stutters, conks out.

"You gotta be fucking kidding. I'm not made of money!"

He gets out. Pops the hood.

"I just took it to José," he says. "I wish Bob was alive. I think the new guy's ripping me off."

I ask him if it's the battery.

"I don't know," he says. "Maybe. They go so fast."

My father flags down a guy walking to his car and asks him if he could jump us. The guy agrees, pulls his car over, then hooks the wires to our battery and his. He tells my father to give it a try. He revs the engine. Nothing. Tries it again. Nothing.

"Might not be the battery," the guy says. "Wish I could be more help."

We call AAA and wait for them to arrive. I have class in the morning.

The tow truck comes forty-five minutes later. The guy attaches a heavy metal hook onto the back and loads the car up onto a lift. We get into the cab of the truck, and he drives us to the closest auto shop, where we find out that our catalytic converter is busted. They have to keep it overnight.

"We live two hours away," my father says.

The guy's hands are covered in oil, a slick, shiny black. He wipes them off on a rag and tells us there're a few motels in town and points us in the right direction.

My father and I walk along the side of some hilly upstate road, surrounded by rust-colored leaves and shrubs on either side.

"You look worried," he says.

"No," I say. "I just don't want to miss a class."

"You're too young to be so worried," he says. "We'll get you home."

He pauses.

"It's always somethin' with these old cars, isn't it? If this isn't broken, it's something else. I'd like to just buy a new one. Not even brand-new. Just sort of new."

We make it about a mile before my father's back starts to hurt, and we stop to rest for a moment on a curb. The smell of chimney wood smoke is in the air. It's a pretty time to be up here.

"When I was in the army," he says, "I could run eight miles. Best shape of my life."

I help him stand, and we keep walking up a road until we see a long driveway that leads to a hotel. The lobby looks expensive.

A man in a nice suit greets us from behind a marble counter. My father asks him for a room.

It's $215 a night.

"Say it again," my father says.

"Two hundred and fifteen dollars for a nonsmoking room," the man behind the counter says.

"Two hundred and fifteen dollars? Last time I stayed in a hotel it was 1948. It cost two dollars and fifteen cents."

The man tells us there's a cheaper motel down the road.

It's getting late, and the sky is turning a cloudy shade of sapphire. Most of the roads don't have street signs, and there are no streetlights, just an occasional porch lamp.

My father talks about his act.

"If I could dance, that would really put a sexy spin on the act. I see those guys on *Dancing with the Stars*...man, they can move."

We turn down another winding road. My father starts to hold his back again.

"Are we going north?" I ask him.

He snorts. "You're asking me? I have no sense of direction. If I'm in the basement of our house, I can't even tell you where the front of the house is. Holy shit, you shoulda seen me in the army. They used to say, 'Louie, we're gonna send you over to Germany,' and I'd say, 'I think you're safer if I'm here.'"

My father tells his stories. I've heard them before. I know

his pauses. His inflections. But I let him tell them over again. Someday, I think, I'll be happy I did.

It's been dark for a while when we admit we're lost.

The houses look the same. We cross a stone-and-concrete bridge and go up a slight hill to find what seems like some sort of main street. Two Hasidic Jews pass in black hats and long black coats and twirly sideburns and long beards.

My father throws his hands up in the air. "*Now* where the fuck are we?"

On the other side of the road, more Hasidic Jews go by. Four of them.

"Go ask 'em if they know where there's a motel around here."

I walk up to the group. Say hello. Ask them if by chance they know of a motel in the area.

They all look at each other and shake their heads.

My father walks up beside me. "What about a place to eat? A pizza place?"

One of the guys says yes, up and over the hill. Jimmy's Pizza, some of the best.

Jimmy's Pizza is empty except for a little boy wearing a yarmulke. On the wall there's a photo of Jimmy with Governor Pataki.

"Give us two cheese, an orange Slice, and whatever he wants..."

I order a Coke.

We sit at a table covered with a red-and-white checkered tablecloth.

"Did I tell you I've been going with one of these broads at one of the nursing homes?"

"No."

"Her name's Eleanor. Forgets everything. A real pain in the ass. I take her out to lunch after a show. Usually Chinese. I figure maybe she'll leave me something in her will."

I take a bite.

"Your mother never had another boyfriend?"

"No," I say. "I don't think she wanted that for us, you know? Another guy around."

"She should," he says. "She's still young. Pretty. Smart as a whip. I remember she went for that job at Olen's Rent-a-Car. She had to memorize all those cars and models in a week. And she came home and studied every night and had it down like that." He snaps his fingers. "And I thought, she's gonna own the fuckin' place at this rate."

He folds his pizza and takes a bite.

"And shrewd, boy, let me tell ya. I used to tell Katz, or whoever my lawyer was back then, I used to say, 'You can't beat her,' and sure enough she'd get up on that stand in front of that judge and make a fool out of him."

His eyes glaze over.

"You don't know the half of what went on, kiddo. I never wanted to get married. My brothers, they married the first girl on the block. That wasn't me. I get bored too easy. I was never the type to get married. You know, I never remembered your mother's birthday. All those years. I didn't know what she wanted. What she needed. I was just never any good at it."

"Would you do it over again?" I ask. "Knowing how it all went?"

"If it meant having you and Stevie...of course."

He takes a sip of his orange Slice. Adds more red pepper to his pizza. "You know, when I had Stevie, I was—what?—early sixties? I never expected kids. But when I held him for the first time, man, oh, man, I swear I never loved anything as much as I loved him. This little person I barely knew. And when your mother told me she was pregnant again, with you, I thought to myself, I thought, how the hell am I gonna love another kid? I love this one so much. But it just happens. Your heart makes room. It's not like anything else."

He takes a bite. And with his mouth half full, he says, "Your mother, I'm sure she feels the same way. For whatever else we didn't have, for all the bullshit and fighting and all the hell we went through, we got you guys out of it."

We leave a couple of dollars as a tip and set out again. It's colder now. It's well after ten when we come upon an old gas station with a motel behind it.

"Would you look at that?!" he says.

Inside the lobby there's a gray-haired man behind a counter. "Lookin' for a room?"

"Guess so," my father says. "We've been walking for hours."

My father asks him how far we are from the nursing home, the auto shop, the places we came from.

The guy says less than a mile.

"Shit, we've been walking in circles."

"Two beds?"

My father nods.

"How does seventy-eight dollars plus tax sound?"

"Gee, it's a new world," he says. "Guess we gotta do it."

He pays in cash.

The hotel has free HBO. We're watching Bill Maher. He's making fun of Dick Cheney shooting some guy with a hunting rifle. I've never seen my father in a motel room before. He looks out of place.

I'm sprawled out on my bed with books and papers and worksheets around me, doing some homework. *Real Sex 24* is on next. I can't believe they're already on the twenty-fourth installment.

"Can I ask you something?" I say.

"Sure," he says and turns off Bill Maher.

"Did you ever feel like, I dunno, you were just…"

I'm afraid to say the words out loud. I start again.

"It's just… I dunno…"

He interrupts. "You feel like you're constantly shoveling shit against the tide."

"Yeah," I say. "I'm just always so worried," I say. "It's like I'm always waiting for a piano to fall out of the sky."

My father laughs. "Kiddo, this is life. Bad things happen." He puts his hand on my shoulder. "And good things will happen, too."

In the morning we wake up early and walk back to the auto shop, where the car is ready for us.

My days at school are long. I'm up early for class, up late in the seventh-floor stacks, where all the poems are. In my psychology class we get our first test back, facedown, and I put it in my backpack without looking. Later, when I'm alone, I dig it out and promise myself I'll keep working hard even if I failed it. I peek and see an A in bright red marker at the top of the page.

I figure there are a few hundred more tests and quizzes and papers ahead of me, each one its own obstacle. But for now it's one at a time.

I spend my days researching graduate schools.

I get to know the schools well. The faculties. I memorize

their stats as though they were baseball players. Make lists of my favorite writers and where they studied, where they teach. I carry their books around in my backpack.

I read an interview with Stephen Dunn in which he talks about getting rejected by Columbia University. Fuck those guys, I think.

I come home from school at the end of the semester to see my father cooking in the kitchen.

"I'm making pasta e fagioli," he says.

"I got straight As," I tell him.

"Oh!" he shouts. "See, you worry for nothing."

And later I hear him bragging on the phone to a friend.

Long Island is muggy in July. Summer classes start the next week. I visit Elizabeth in her office, and we talk about books. She lets me borrow some of hers. I let her borrow some of mine. I get bills from the school. The car is full of financial aid applications and scholarship applications and Sallie Mae bills and Citibank bills.

Come fall, I declare my major in philosophy. I work alone at a communal table at the back of the library, my books and papers and old quizzes sprawled around me. When I don't understand a paragraph, I make myself write it out in longhand to get it into my stubborn brain any way I can.

My cell phone vibrates against the cold desk. It's a number I don't recognize.

"Hello?" I whisper.

"Kiddo? It's Dad."

"Hey, what's up? Where are you calling from?"

"I'm at the hospital."

He tells me he's okay before I have the chance to ask.

I go into the next room and ask him what happened.

"I was doing a job. Good show, by the way. About a hundred people—"

"Okay, and—"

"And I started feeling real weak toward the end, and I collapsed. They think it's probably low blood sugar. They gave me a cookie."

He tells me he feels okay, that the hospital is just up the road from my school. He says he can go home when they're finished running a bunch of tests. I tell him I'll be there soon.

Later that week I arrive home from school, and my father's watching Emeril Lagasse cooking chicken cacciatore on the TV.

He turns it off when I come in. "Sit down," he says.

"Uh-oh," I say and smile. "Did I do something wrong?"

"You? *Never*," he says. He looks like he might start crying. "I got the test results back. The blockage is malignant."

"Cancer?"

"Yes."

I breathe in. Exhale.

"Okay. What does that mean?"

"It's still pretty small. They're gonna cut it out. I have to go in for a procedure Wednesday."

"Well, that's good," I say. "I mean, as long as they can get it out it'll be fine."

"You know, I'm laying here waiting for you to get home, and I'm thinking, is this it for me? Hearing him say cancer, it was a big wake-up call, really made me realize, you know, I'm not gonna be here forever."

He continues.

"I don't feel sick; I don't feel old. But I look in the mirror sometimes and I realize, Louie, you're old. Like, the people on this block, our neighbors, they only know me as the old guy. But I had a whole other life. One you don't even really know. But you live long enough to see everybody die, and your stories go with them."

He pauses, then goes on.

"I sit here thinking back over my life, the army, that resort I worked at with my brothers upstate, singing on the radio, working at the transit authority, and I think, did I really do all that shit? Did I do all those jobs? Did I really sleep with that broad in Kansas while her husband was in the next room?"

I laugh.

"Are you scared?" I ask him.

"Nah."

"Got any wisdom for me?"

"Wisdom?"

"Yeah, you're old," I say and smile. "You must have something."

"Kiddo, I feel like I've been alive so long that I know less now than I ever did."

The VA hospital in the Bronx is a large white medical complex surrounded by run-down brick apartment buildings. I knock on the door of my father's room and push the door open. His doctor, a broad-shouldered Indian man with a serious mustache, is checking my father's chart while my father tells him a joke:

"Guy goes into a bar, gets drunk, and throws up all over himself. 'Oh, no!' he says. 'My wife's gonna kill me. She said if I threw up on another new shirt she'd kick me out.'

" 'Don't worry,' says the bartender. 'Just do what I do. Put a twenty-dollar bill in your shirt pocket and tell her the neighborhood drunk threw up on you and gave you twenty dollars to pay for the dry cleaning.'

"So the man goes home and tells his wife the story.

" 'Okay,' she says. 'That's understandable. Except there's forty dollars here.'

" 'Yeah,' says the man. 'He shit in my pants, too.' "

The doctor smiles.

My father's clothes are on a plastic chair beside him, and he's wearing a paper gown that doesn't cover his pasty white legs. *Jeopardy!* is playing on the small TV bolted to the ceiling. *Wheel of Fortune* is on next.

I move his clothes aside and take a seat.

A Jamaican nurse comes in to give my father some medicine. He tells her the food is shit, asks if she can sneak him some stuffed shells. She laughs, tells him to get out of here.

"God, these mashed potatoes," he says to me. "Hard as a fuckin' rock."

"So what's the deal?" I ask him.

"They're going to operate tomorrow," he says. "I gotta drink a gallon of some liquid. Tastes like I'm drinking gasoline. I was drinking it earlier, thinking, they couldn't have made it orange-flavored? Something? It's worse than the cancer. But it's supposed to clean me out before they go in."

"And that's tomorrow?"

He nods and starts eating a small cup of applesauce. "How do you fuck up applesauce? Jeez. You'd think for what they charge you they could get you some decent food. I always knew there was a reason I've stayed out of hospitals. Look at this shit," he says, picking at the neck of his paper gown. "It doesn't matter if you're Joe Schmo or Sinatra, we all end up in these paper gowns. I go down the hall to take a leak, and every nurse in the place sees my ass."

I tell him about my philosophy class today. We're learning about Descartes. And my science class is harder than I thought. I'm not so good at science. We have a quiz tomorrow I'm nervous about. He tells me it'll be okay.

Visiting hours are only until 9:00 p.m., but the nurse lets me stay later as long as the other bed stays empty.

I brought playing cards with me, and I deal. We play 500 rummy.

"Did you ever have a best friend growing up?"

"You were named after him," he says. "Kenny O'Brien. Used to ride around Jamaica, Queens, together as kids. Buy a Coke for a nickel. We lost touch after the army. Last I heard he moved to Vermont or one of those states that sounds like Vermont."

"I have a best friend back in Arizona," I tell him. "He got into heroin a few years ago. Just heard he got back from rehab, but it didn't work. He's already using again."

"Jesus," he says. "Kids can't kill themselves fast enough."

"I was thinking I should talk to him."

"What do you say? You can't reason with people on that shit. It's like your mother with the drink. It's like being chained to a fucking volcano. You need to worry about you, kiddo. Don't go jumping in the water trying to save the day. They'll drown you and not think twice."

He shuffles the cards and deals me another hand.

"You nervous about tomorrow?" I ask him.

He shakes his head.

"You know, playing cards like this, it reminds me of my

father. I used to call him Pop. He would've loved you so much, boy, let me tell you. Good guy, funny. Smoked like a chimney. Everybody did. And one day he goes to the doctor, and the doctor says, 'One more, Francis, one more cigarette, and you're dead.' And just like that he quit. Never had another puff."

I discard an eight of spades and pick up another card from the deck.

"But it was too late. He was in the hospital not long after. Emphysema. I'll never forget seeing him there. It didn't even look like him. I never wanted you to see me like that. That's no way to remember your pop."

He picks up from the pile.

"It's funny...when you're young you spend your life trying to convince yourself you're not like your parents. And then, every now and then, you'll do something a certain way, some mannerism, or you'll say something. When our car broke down upstate, I remember I hit the wheel and said, 'I'm not made of money!' And I caught myself and thought, Gee, Louie, you just sounded like Pop. When you're young and it happens, it drives you crazy. And then you live long enough, and it makes you smile a little."

He wipes a tear from his eyelashes with the back of his hand.

"That's a nice part of life," he says.

chapter 18

It's 3:00 a.m.

I open my eyes. I thought I heard the house phone.

It takes me a second to realize I fell asleep on the couch with the lights and TV on. The *Sex and the City* DVD menu plays on a loop.

I close my eyes just before the phone rings again.

I sit up and look at the digital clock on my cell phone. It's 3:04 a.m. What the fuck?

I grab the phone off the receiver. "Hello?"

"Yes, hello, is this Kenneth Porpora, please?"

"This is him."

"I am calling from the veterans' hospital. About your father, Louis."

"Okay," I say, my brain clouded with sleep. "Is he okay?"

"Um ... I'm afraid he's taken a turn for the worse."

I freeze for a moment. "What does that mean?"

"Can you come in to the hospital, please?"

"Wait, what happened?"

"I'm afraid I can't give that information out over the phone. You'll have to come in."

"You can't give me that information over the phone?"

"I'm sorry, sir."

"Is he alive?"

"Sir, I cannot give that information over the phone."

The hospital is about an hour from our house with no traffic on the Long Island Expressway.

The car's weak headlights barely light the empty roads, but I go ninety the whole time and speed into the empty hospital parking lot. I rush into the lobby, down white hallways, turn a corner, and see a man in a white coat.

"Can I help you, sir?"

"My name is Kenneth Porpora," I say, and he pauses for a moment and says, "Oh," with the sorriest eyes, and tells me to follow him back into the hallway, where I'm met by the doctor from yesterday.

"This is Louis Porpora's son," the man says to the doctor.

The doctor walks toward me and takes off his glasses. "Your father is no more," he says without blinking.

I look through him.

"He's dead?"

He nods.

My stomach feels like a waterbed. A memory flashes in front of me. I'm three years old, climbing to the top of the tree house my father had built for us and falling off backwards, twelve feet at least. I get the wind knocked out of me. My father picks me up, holds me, asks me if I'm okay. And I cry on his shoulder.

Here, now, I get the wind knocked out of me again.

I walk down the hallway. Breathe deeply, run my hands through my hair. Hold on to the back of my neck. Breathe.

I walk back to the doctor.

"What happened?" I ask.

"I don't know, ya know?" another guy says with a Brooklyn accent. Not the doctor. A nurse, maybe. An assistant. An orderly. "Ya know, he got through the surgery all right, was doing all right, we were talking about the Mets, and I remember he was talking about...ah...who was their relief pitcher?...you know, the one who used to always blow the game?"

"John Franco?"

"Yeah, Franco! He was talking about how they used to always bring out Franco in the ninth and he'd always blow the whole goddamn game. And then outta nowhere—*bam!*—heart attack."

It doesn't seem real. I feel like I should protest. He's still in there. I should demand they do something to save him. As long as he's here, there's something we can do.

But they're already talking about him in the past tense. The decision's been made without me.

"You're his grandson?" the guy asks me.

"His son," I say.

He nods solemnly. The doctor stands silently beside him.

"So now what?" I ask him. "That's it? He just died, and that's it?"

"We have his stuff. I can go grab it for you."

He returns a minute later with an oversize plastic bag holding my father's dirty blue jeans, a shopping list in the back pocket, his striped polo shirt, his wallet, which contains a five-dollar bill and seven singles, and his house keys.

He hands it to me and tells me he's sorry.

I thank him and walk back to the elevator and press the button for the lobby.

I have to call my brother.

I have to call my mother.

How the fuck am I gonna tell them?

I dial my brother's number first. It's 2:00 a.m. in Arizona, but he picks up.

"Steve?"

"What the fuck? Everything okay? Daddy okay?"

He's been waiting for this call since he was in kindergarten.

"No," I say. My jaw quivers. "He died."

Dead air on the phone.

"Kenny."

He never says my name.

"I'm sorry," I tell him.

"Kenny, no."

I can hear his voice break. I can hear him crying. I'm not sure I've ever heard him cry.

"Kenny. What the fuck? Are you sure? What did they say?"

"They said he got through the surgery okay and was talking to the guy next to him about the Mets and how much John Franco sucks, and then he had a massive heart attack. Out of nowhere."

"John Franco?" he says.

"I know," I say.

We're silent for a bit.

"You still here?"

He says yes with a cracked voice. I tell him I'm getting into the elevator and I might lose him. The metallic doors close. I see my reflection again. We stop on some odd-numbered floor.

A man in a white coat wheels some trays of food onto the elevator and smiles at me. We ride down to the lobby together.

"You still there?" I ask him.

"Yeah."

"Kenny...we have to tell Mommy," he says.

"I know."

"I'll do it," he says.

"Okay," I say.

"He didn't even get to see the end of the fucking *Sopranos*!" he says and starts crying again.

"I know," I say. "I was just thinking that."

I stay on the phone with him as I get into my car. It's early morning now, and I hear garbage trucks.

"Fuck. I have to call into work, tell them I'm not coming in. We have to get to you somehow. Like, today."

"Yeah, I have class in a few hours," I say.

"I'm going to call Mommy," he says. "I'll call you back."

He says, "I love you, Kenny."

I don't remember the last time he said it, but it's not something we do. And I say, "I love you, too."

I start my father's car and pull out of the parking lot. I drive through the gritty Bronx streets, through dirty tunnels and past graffitied street signs, a plastic bag with my father's clothes and wallet and house keys beside me on the passenger seat. I don't really know where I'm going. I follow street signs until I have to pull over and roll down my window to ask strangers for directions.

It's almost six. I have class in two hours.

I finally find the Long Island Expressway. The traffic is backed up from the tollbooth. I don't want to spend the cash in my father's wallet, so I pull through the window and tell the woman in the booth I don't have the five dollars. She tells me to pull over to the side of the road.

I pull over to the right. Lay my head back against the headrest and close my eyes. A traffic cop knocks on my window. I roll it down, and he asks me for my driver's license. I tell him I don't have my wallet with me.

"Driving without a license?"

"My father just died," I say. "I rushed out here."

He looks at me. "Okay," he says.

He hands me a piece of paper, asks me to write down my address.

"You're still gonna give me a ticket, huh?"

He nods and writes it up. "Sorry to hear about your dad," he says.

I walk through Hofstra's campus toward the brick building all the way in the back, up the stairs, and into the lobby, where Elizabeth's office is.

Her door is open.

She's typing at her desk, her face hidden by books. I walk around her desk, and she sees me.

"Oh, hi, Kenny," she says. "I'm actually putting this test together for my first-period class...did you need something?"

"Um...my father died this morning."

"Oh, my God." She stands up, hugs me, pulls out a chair, and tells me to sit down.

"Tea," she says. "You need some tea. I have chamomile. Chamomile?"

I nod.

I hate chamomile tea, but it doesn't matter right now.

She gets hot water in a cup, digs through her collection

of teas, and tears open the chamomile and dunks it in the water.

"I'm here for you," she says. "I have to finish writing this test before my class starts, but I'm here. I'm listening."

She puts her hand on mine to make sure I hear her and types with the other.

I sip the tea. It's awful.

"What's the test?" I ask her.

"We're reading *The Kite Runner*," she says, then drops her voice to a conspiratorial whisper. "I don't think any of them are actually reading it. Is the tea okay?"

I nod.

She's waiting for me to talk.

"He went into the hospital for a surgery. He had a tumor in his colon. And they removed it. And I called yesterday to ask if he made it through okay."

She's typing, glancing over at me and then at her computer screen, nodding.

"And they said yes, he was fine. I could pick him up today. And then they called in the middle of the night. Said he took a turn for the worse. I asked if he was okay, and they said they couldn't tell me on the phone. So I drove out to the Bronx, and the doctor told me he was dead."

She stops typing.

"Oh, Kenny, I'm so sorry. Have you talked to your mom?"

"Yes."

"Is she okay?"

I nod. "I mean, I don't know. She's flying here right now."

"Okay," she says. "Because you can stay with me. Here in this office. You are welcome in my home. If you need a place to sleep. Anything."

I thank her.

"He was talking about the Mets right before he died," I tell her.

"I was working on my PhD during the 1986 World Series," she says. "I'd be working in one room and listening to the game from the TV in the other room. And when they won I'm in the middle of this quiet study area where all these academics are working, and I'm jumping up and down!"

Every few minutes it hits me again like a wave through my stomach, and I catch my breath.

"What should I do about my classes?" I ask her.

"I can talk to your teachers for you. You need to take some time off."

"My family's never been very good at this stuff, you know? School. Finishing what we start. Stuff like that."

I sniffle, and she hands me a tissue.

"I remember when my mother's brother died. My uncle Carter. My mother was trying to go back to school. And she was doing pretty good. And then he died, and she took some time off. And she never went back. I don't want that to happen to me."

She leans forward.

"If you don't want it to happen," she says, "then don't let it happen. You are not your history. You are you. You have the power to make that decision. But you need to take some time off right now, okay?"

I wipe my nose.

"And you'll be back."

Her class is starting, and she has to go. "You can stay in my office," she says.

"It's okay," I say. "I might go sit at the Dunkin' Donuts across the street."

She goes into her purse and hands me a neatly folded twenty-dollar bill.

"Nope," I say.

"Yes," she says, and it's already in my hand. "Actually..." She hands me another twenty. "Take it. Get yourself some coffee."

She hugs me again.

It's already night when I pull into our driveway. The daylight gives up more easily this time of year. The curtains are drawn, and it already feels like he died a month ago. Inside the house I turn on a table lamp. There are dishes in the sink. His song sheets are scattered on the table. The life he accumulated is cluttered in corners, in closets, in dresser drawers; his eyeglasses, grocery lists, loose change, playing cards.

I go into his bedroom, which used to be my parents' bedroom, and I sit on the bed I used to crawl into when my imagination got the best of me in the dark. His calendar of nursing-home shows is thumbtacked to the wall, his handwriting in the small boxes. Black-and-white photos of his parents on the desk next to a photo of me, four years old, chubby cheeks and bushy hair and a pout on my face. A school photo of my brother when he was going through his flattop phase. I open a dresser drawer: black socks, jockey shorts, handkerchiefs, and inside one of his socks, a bottle of black hair dye.

An old *Newsday* with Cal Ripken Jr. on the front page the day after he broke Lou Gehrig's record for most consecutive games played. He must've thought it'd be worth something someday.

There's a crucifix on his nightstand. Rosary beads. Some

scattered photos of him as a young man in the army, not much older than I am now. I look like him.

I rub the tears from my cheeks.

In his closet, his clothes and the clothes he inherited from his dead brothers. Everything smells like him. I reach into one of his pants pockets and find a crumpled piece of paper. I unfold it.

It's the punch line of a joke scribbled in blue pen.

Hear about the Polish-Italian? He made himself an offer he couldn't understand . . .

I crumple it back up again.

It's been raining. The streets are slick and reflective. There's a pungent, earthy smell to the air.

I pull into the Applebee's parking lot, tiptoe through puddles and wet pavement, and step inside. Flat-screen TVs on all sides are playing the Mets game. My mother and brother are together in a back booth. My mother slides out of the booth, and I bend down to hug her and kiss her on the cheek before I take a seat beside my brother.

My mother is keeping her eyes as wide as she can to keep from crying.

"I'm sorry," she says, and puts her hand on mine, and I nod to say it's okay.

I look at my brother. He usually makes jokes to keep sadness away, and when instead he asks me if I'm okay, it makes it all the more real.

The place explodes in disappointed cries of "Oh!"

The Mets just left two men on base.

"Oh, they're fuckin' pathetic," my mother says. "Let's pay him another twenty million dollars to swing like a fuckin' girl."

"How was the flight?" I ask.

My brother shrugs.

"I'm so exhausted," he says. "I've been up since you called me."

"I can't believe that was today," I say.

"Tell me about it," my mother says. "I've been up since four."

The waitress comes around to ask me if she can take my drink order.

I say no. There are half-eaten appetizers on the table. Fried mozzarella sticks and chicken wings and onion rings. My mother asks me if I want anything, and I say I'm not hungry.

"You need to eat," she says.

She scoots out of the booth, says she's going to the little girls' room, asks us to watch her purse.

"She's been talking nonstop since five a.m.," my brother says. "Like, I'm not exaggerating—nonstop. I even timed her at one point."

"She's just sad," I say.

"Oh, it wasn't about Daddy. It was about—seriously—anything but him."

"You know she's never been good at this."

"Whatever. I'm worried about her seeing the house. I'm afraid she's gonna lose her shit."

They follow me home in their rental car, but I get there first.

I fiddle with the house keys and open the door. Turn on the lights.

My mother walks in behind me. Then my brother. It's the first time we've been together in this house since it was foreclosed on twelve years ago.

My mother walks down the hall, past the patched-up holes in the wall, into her old bedroom. I look at my brother.

"Where did you guys go?" I ask him.

"We made a stop at a convenience store," he says.

I know what that means.

"He's such a disgusting old man," my mother mutters under her breath as she walks back into the kitchen.

"Mom—"

"Don't fucking 'Mom' me…this is disgusting, bag-man shit. It's like a fuckin' halfway house in here. Mold on the plates. Look at these fuckin' floors!"

"Okay, but can we worry about the floors later?"

She's not listening to me.

"He was always such a disgusting fucking pedophile."

"Kenny and I are gonna go for a ride," my brother says and grabs the keys to his rental car. Walks quickly out of the house, and I follow him.

We drive along the same roads we used to ride our bikes on. Past our old school, a nursing home where my father once sang, grocery stores, and local bank branches. My brother drives us down a desolate, dead-end road and pulls the car into the U-shaped cul-de-sac.

We sit there with the headlights on.

"I just did not want to be in that house right now," he says. "I was thinking about all this sad shit on the plane. All the stuff he wasn't going to be around to see. And, like, little things…remember how he saved all those soda-can tabs for you for that school project?"

"Yeah," I say.

"And now what? We just throw them away? And like, how hard he worked to get the house back, and now he's dead. It's just bullshit…

"I remember sitting in front of that judge and those lawyers and telling them I wanted to live with Mommy instead of with him. And telling them about how dirty his house was and how we were on food stamps and how he took us to the dollar movie theater and bought us clothes at the thrift store, and he looked like he was going to break into pieces."

He goes on.

"And fuckin' Mommy. Coaching me on what to say. I was ten fucking years old."

He looks away from me, out the window.

"I remember being in kindergarten, and when he was late picking me up, I'd think he was dead. Because he was always so old."

We sit there for a moment.

"You know what's even worse than it hurting so bad?" I say. "Knowing one day it won't hurt anymore."

"Yeah," he says. "One day he'll have been dead longer than we ever knew him."

When we pull in front of the house, I can hear my mother yelling inside, fighting with ghosts.

I open the front door.

She's in her nightgown, putting a bottle under the kitchen sink. She slams the cabinet door closed. Grabs her full glass.

"You both make me sick, you little faggots!" she yells. "Crying over that piece of shit. The two a you: *My daddy! My daddy!* Who gives a fuck? The old prick is finally dead. My life can finally begin. Bye-bye, Louie, bye-bye. It's party time! Louie the pedophile rapist is dead! Are you in hell, Louie?"

She takes a sip of her drink.

"Stick a fuckin' tube up his ass and fill him with formaldehyde and dump him in the ground, where he belongs! Lived with his mother till he was forty fuckin' years old. She used to call him Susie Mary. Him and your uncle Danny. Probably sucked each other's cocks.

"My father should've kicked him in his balls. He should've said, 'Why the fuck are you hanging around a nineteen-year-old girl?' He was a fuckin' pussy, too. All these pussy men. Just like the two of you."

My brother tells her to shut the fuck up.

"Nice way to talk to your mother," she says.

The vodka is like quicksand. She quickly gets louder, meaner.

"Why should I, Stevie? Is the Puerto Rican downstairs gonna move out? God forbid Louie doesn't have the extra money coming in. Oh, that's right. He doesn't need it anymore. He's dead. Louie and his saggy balls are in hell with the devil. Hallelujah. Jumpin' around on stage like a fuckin' queer. *Look at me, I'm a star. Love me. Love me.* Why don't you go eat a meatball hero on his fucking grave. He bashed my fuckin' eardrum in! He stole my house! He stole my life!"

My brother runs up to her with his fist cocked.

"Somebody ought to break your fucking jaw!" he yells.

My mother backs up in fear.

He stops himself. Holds his fist, clenching it.

"Go ahead, Stevie. Hit me. Hit me like your father hit me. You gonna break my eardrum, too?"

She continues her tirade. Fills her glass up again.

I go to her, and I can smell the vodka on her warm breath. In a whisper, I tell her she's breaking my heart and ask her if she could please stop.

"Oh, what's the matter, Kenny? Mr. Melodrama. You gonna cry for that old piece of shit that raped you? I know he did. He raped you and your brother."

I can see only her mouth.

"He stuck his fingers in your ass and you probably liked it. Didn't you? Fucking queer. Little traitor. Talking to him after what he did to me. Why don't you go suck his dead dick in hell?!"

I cock my head back and spit into my mother's face. My white, dry spit splatters all over her. She's shocked into quiet. Wide, pained eyes and a face that looks like it could crack into pieces. She looks pathetic. The regret builds in my chest, in my neck, spreading hot sadness into my ears and behind my eyes. I want to take it back. I want to say I'm sorry and hug her and cry on her shoulder. But I don't. I just stand there and stare at her. And I watch her crumble into tears, wipe my spit off her face with her nightgown. And then she explodes into another fit of piercing screams.

I go into my father's room and lie on his bed. His pillow smells like him.

I cry on his bed. Sob. Scream into the pillow until my head hurts.

And I fall asleep.

I wake up with a headache. I have no idea where I am. I look at the clock. It's late. Early. One a.m. It's been a few hours. My mother is sitting on the bed beside me in the dark.

"I'm very sorry about your father, Kenneth," she says. "You know what he said to me the night my sister Gina died?"

I can't see her face.

"He said, 'I hope they don't cremate her. She has so much alcohol in her blood they'll burn down New York City.' But he was your father, and I know you loved him."

She gets up. My eyes slowly adjust. I can see her silhouette moving. She goes to the door, says good night. Asks me if I want her to leave the hallway light on.

I tell her she can turn it off, and she does.

My mother takes the flowers and balloons out of the backseat of the rental car as my brother and I approach the door of the funeral home, where a man holds the door open for us.

"You're here for Louis Porpora?" he asks us. Somebody needs to see his body before they close the casket, and I tell him I will. My brother says he wants to see him, too.

The last time I saw my father he was in a hospital gown talking about all those things he was going to do when he got home because he didn't know he was going to die. I'm not sure I want to see him dead, but I follow this somber man into a viewing room, and there's my father, wearing his favorite blue dress shirt, looking like he's just dozed off for a minute. He looks handsome with his hair combed back.

"He looks okay?" the man asks.

There's something comforting about seeing him. He's right there, like nothing's changed.

"Yes," I tell him.

They close the casket and open the doors.

My mother looks pretty in black slacks and a black jacket. She thanks the funeral director cautiously and puts the flowers on the table.

"I remember when my father died," she says. "They wanted me to see him. And of course, Kerry the Bitch had to have her melodrama. God forbid we go a minute without her auditioning for *General Hospital*."

"Mom—"

"Okay, I'm just saying, she's a bitch. She's my sister, and I love her, but she's a bitch."

Old neighbors arrive. A few new ones. Some distant cousins in their midforties with children of their own, who tell me we met when I was two.

"Who's the one who played the clarinet in band?" they ask, and my brother says he was the one. They tell us our father was very proud of us.

A man my father used to sing with years ago tells us his version of stories.

My mother tells the story of how they met, in a New York City nightclub where my father was singing. It was her sister who first saw him on the stage and thought my mother would find him cute, so she came back the next night with her. My father asked her name from the stage and dedicated a song to her. My mother was shy, embarrassed.

We tell his stories for him.

His detailed advice on buying cold cuts at the deli.

The handkerchief he kept in his pocket in case somebody had to sneeze.

Quietly, my brother and I tell our own stories to each other.

"Remember he had us make him a list of Julia Roberts movies just so he wouldn't accidentally rent one?"

We have a voice for my father, and we do it back and forth, though it doesn't sound much like him.

The next morning we cross the cemetery to reach a deep, rectangular hole in the ground beside the headstones of my grandparents. A robust priest with a violent lisp gives a eulogy over the noise from the main street. My father was possibly the least patriotic soldier ever to have been drafted into

World War II and spent his tenure having threesomes in Kansas instead of fighting Nazis, so his formal military send-off makes me giggle.

"Louith wath a hero to uth all!" the priest says, and my brother and I start cracking up.

"We honor him today for hith brave military servith and for the way he defended hith country in timeth of peril!"

My brother starts mimicking him. "Louith wath a coward who loved puthy more than hith country!"

Now my mother's laughing, too.

The man finishes his eulogy.

His coffin is draped in a flag. A soldier folds the flag and hands it to my mother. As they then begin to lower his coffin into the ground, his death reoccurs to me, suddenly feeling too permanent, too real. I walk to the edge of the hole and lay a flower on his coffin. My brother does the same. And we walk back through a maze of slate-gray headstones and leave him there alone.

I say good-bye to my mother and brother at the airport and drive myself back to the house, which is too quiet.

The first few hours after they leave are the hardest. His clothes need to be packed up and given to the church. His paperwork needs to be boxed up and stored away. I need to go to school and continue with my life.

The next morning I'm heading to class when I run into Elizabeth.

"You know, I was thinking about calling you, but I didn't know if I should," she says. "How are you doing?"

I tell her I'm okay.

"And what class are you off to?"

"Philosophy."

"Okay," she says. She smiles sadly at me. Or maybe proudly; I can't tell. "You know where my office is."

It takes a long time to settle the life of a dead person. Mail still arrives with his name on it. Bills. Bank statements. I come home from school to the blinking red light on the answering machine.

"Hi, Lou, this is Rosemary from the Glen Cove nursing home. I have you scheduled for tomorrow at nine a.m. Just calling to confirm you'll be here."

I rub my hands over my face. I hate calling the nursing homes he used to sing for to tell them he's gone.

Soon the April cherry blossoms begin to bloom. It's only been six months, but it feels longer. I work alone at nearby diners with empty sugar packets and books scattered across the table. I eat dinner at our favorite restaurant, order the same thing every time, look at the empty booth across from me. I wander the aisles of Blockbuster, rent a movie to pass the time. At home I waste time on the Internet, falling down the rabbit hole of Wikipedia hyperlinks. The Guns N' Roses article leads to the Slash article leads to the Les Paul article. Les Paul is still alive. I didn't know that. Scroll to the bottom of the page and click on a link that takes me to an article about Les Paul. It says he plays every Monday night at a club in Manhattan. Daddy would love that, I think.

I get out of my chair and head into the living room.

"Hey, Dad," I yell before I can catch myself.

Goddamn it.

I stand in our quiet living room and let it occur to me.

chapter 19

It's late spring when my mother comes back to New York and we hammer a FOR SALE sign into the soft dirt of our front yard. It was a long, snowy winter, and in February, when the pipes froze and burst without a sound and our basement flooded with freezing cold water the color of stale coffee, I called my mother, and she told me it was time to sell the house. I pick her up from the airport in my father's car, and we drive together to the house. The bathroom floor is caving in. The ceilings are sagging. The pipes are old. There's damage from the flood. The house needs work. It's time to let it go.

My mother and I dig through boxes in the basement.

"Oh, my God," she says.

She's holding the label she peeled off a beer bottle in Mexico when they were on their honeymoon.

"How did this survive?"

Most of the papers and magazines down here were ruined in the flood. Most of the photographs, too. We save what we can.

Our house sells quickly to a young couple with a new baby boy. It sells for more money than any of us have ever seen. Because my mother and father were legally separated but technically still married, my mother inherited the money from the house and split it with my brother and me, telling us to be responsible.

I move into a small apartment a few towns over, a cute little studio that's attached to the back of the house of a nice divorcée. I buy some furniture. Now and then I drive by our old house and watch it change. One day it has new aluminum siding and a new roof, a new white fence, and a small addition, and I realize it's not ours anymore.

I'm taking Mark McEvoy's philosophy class.

McEvoy is an Irishman with a dry sense of humor and droopy, bulldog eyes whose brogue makes everything he says funnier than it is. He paces a room of about twenty-five desks and chairs, most of them occupied. Our books are turned to a passage by Camus.

"We left last week talking about Sisyphus. Did we all do the reading?"

Tired heads nod.

"I assign *The Myth of Sisyphus* every year," he says. "Last year—or maybe it was a few years ago now—I had this student raise his hand. He was an athlete. A baseball player, I think. Never spoke much. But anyway, he raises his hand and says…"

McEvoy affects a California surfer-dude accent.

"This Syphilis guy, was he a real person?"

The whole class laughs.

"I assured him that yes, syphilis is very real."

The laughter dies down. McEvoy turns serious.

"What's Camus saying here?"

No hands go up.

He walks through the maze of desks.

"Did we *do* the reading? Were we *out* too late? At the bars? Having a pint? Spreading syphilis, perhaps?"

We laugh again.

A hand goes up in the back.

"He's, like, talking about how absurd life is."

McEvoy writes the word *absurd* on the board.

"Man's futile search for meaning," McEvoy says. "In a world devoid of God! Camus was clearly a very fun man to hang out with—great sense of humor, very easygoing. And how does he depict the absurdity?"

He looks at me. "Ken?"

I answer softly. "He tells a story about Sisyphus, who has been punished and sentenced to a fate of rolling a rock up a hill again and again only to see it fall back down."

McEvoy nods.

"And Camus sees this futile labor as the worst possible punishment," I say.

He looks around at the class. "This idea of rolling this impossible boulder up a hill just to watch it fall again: Can we relate to Sisyphus?"

Some of us nod.

"So what is it that Camus says? I mean, if this is his metaphor for life, and life is meaningless, then why not choose death?"

He looks around the classroom. "Well? What does Camus say about acceptance?"

I raise my hand, halfway.

"He says once Sisyphus accepts his fate, he can find happiness in the struggle."

"Yes," he says. "For Camus, death isn't the answer, but neither is hope."

He looks down at his notebook and reads from it verbatim: "He says, 'The hero of ordinary life is the person who resolutely shoulders the responsibilities that life imposes.'"

He looks up and around. "Camus says, 'Okay, maybe life is absurd. Meaningless. Fine!' But instead of running from that truth with hope or suicide—some do it with religion, some with drugs, some with work, all the many distractions—Camus wants us to feel it, sit with it, see if we can live with it, and still charge forward. It's like he's saying, 'What else could you possibly take from me?' He's saying we have an instinct for life. His acceptance is his revolt."

And he reads the last line of the text: "One must imagine Sisyphus happy."

McEvoy looks around the room. "Do we agree with Camus?"

The kid next to me says, "Sounds like he needs to smoke some weed."

We all laugh.

Every day after school I go to my *Newsday* internship. Elizabeth told me that internships might help me get into Columbia University's graduate program in journalism, so I apply for them all the time. The *Newsday* internship is one I'd applied for twice already. I got it after a short-lived stint at the *Long Island Press,* where I would go a couple of times a week to help research articles. They once forced me to wear a panda costume and hand out newspapers at a high school football game.

Newsday, though, is a different kind of internship. I spend my days, and most nights, in the Bronx or Brooklyn, standing outside yellow-taped crime scenes with reporters who have much more experience than I do. I scribble down everything everybody says and rush back to the office to write stories on deadline.

I say the words "I'm on deadline" as often as I can, even when I'm not. I publish a front-page story on a Saturday, and it's a proud day for me.

I overhear kids in my classes talking about frat parties—*Omigod Michelle so lost her phone at the club!*—and they sound fun, but I don't make any friends during college. I don't have sex, even though I'm supposed to. I write and I study and I daydream myself into a life I'm not sure will ever be possible. And I spend the in-between hours fighting the doubt that inevitably creeps in to remind me of who I am.

My graduate-school applications are due at the end of the fall semester. I make a list of schools I think I can get into. I try to think of ways to make my application stand out, and when I overhear a girl in one of my classes talking about how she just got back from covering the presidential primaries in Iowa, I decide to go to South Carolina to cover that state's primary. I buy a ticket to Charleston with some money I have left from the sale of our house and keep writing stories and hope that the Columbia Journalism School will appreciate my efforts.

I land in Charleston, and I'm immediately lost. I'm not old enough to rent a car, but a classmate of mine used to work at Enterprise, so he pulls some strings to get me one. I drive through the dark streets looking at my printout of MapQuest directions to the hotel where John McCain is having his victory party. And I'm late.

In the lobby, gangs of rabid Republicans are chanting "Mac is back!" as McCain vows to defeat whichever candidate wins the Democratic primary—Senator Clinton or Obama.

In the morning I head south to Columbia. It's chaos inside the Lizard's Thicket when I arrive at 7:00 a.m. The small shack of a diner is crowded with television cameras and reporters and annoyed regulars and harried waitresses screaming orders at fry cooks. The throngs of people erupt in cheers when Bill Clinton walks in, wearing a blinding orange tie, to stump for his wife's presidential bid.

I call my mother from my cell phone, and she picks up.

"Can you hear me?" I ask her.

"Is Bill there?"

"Yeah, it's crazy. Hold on one second."

I inch my way close to him and ask him for a photograph. He poses with me, and a stranger snaps a photo with my camera. He quickly moves on through the crowd.

"I just took a picture with him," I tell her.

"Far out!" she says.

My mother is an unabashed Democrat.

"Hold on," I tell her. I push my way back through the crowd to a spot where Clinton's hobnobbing with some waitresses.

"President Clinton," I call out.

He looks at me.

"Can you say hi to my mom?" I yell.

I hand him my little phone, and he puts it to his ear.

"Hi, there!" he says.

I can hear my mother's scream on the other end. "Ahhhh! You are terrific. And I love your wife."

He tries to hand the phone back to me, but my mother's still talking, so he puts it back to his ear.

"You know, I work at a school cafeteria. It's very hard work, you know?"

"Okay," he says and tries to hand it back, but she's still going.

"...and my Stevie read *The Catcher in the Rye* in third grade."

Finally he doesn't know what to do, and he hands the phone back to me.

At South Carolina State University in Orangeburg, Barack Obama paces back and forth on a stage. He's talking about the economy. Jobs. School. The crowd waves their banners.

"Yes, we can!" they chant.

I arrive back home a few days before my graduate-school applications are due and spend those days at Kinko's photocopying my newspaper clips, my personal essay, my work from South Carolina. I gather my three letters of recommendation for each envelope and seal each one. Each application is accompanied by a check for the one-hundred-dollar application fee. I lay the envelopes on the backseat of my father's car.

My phone buzzes. It's *Newsday*, calling with an assignment to cover a shooting in the Bronx.

My editor asks me if I can make it, and I tell her yes. I always say yes.

I drive to the Bronx and head into a dilapidated building in the Morrisania neighborhood. The *New York Post* is already downstairs. An *Eyewitness News* van is outside.

But nobody's talking.

Family members of the victim keep asking us to leave. We stay and wait until the night gets colder. The assignment becomes a stakeout, and I wait for my editors at the newspaper to tell me I can go home.

"Anything?" my editor asks.

"No," I tell her. Still nothing.

"All right," she says. "Wait until ten, and if there's still nothing, you can go."

At ten o'clock I walk down the block and around the corner and see an empty space where I parked my father's car.

"No, no, no, no, no!"

I run up and down the block.

"Fuck, fuck, fuck..."

I check the street sign to make sure I have the right block. I check it again. Maybe it was towed. But the sign says I'm allowed to park there.

I run up and down the streets.

And when I remember my applications in the backseat, I put my hands on my head and feel like the wind's been knocked out of me.

"Motherfucker!"

I find a police car and tell the officers what happened. They don't give a shit. Ask me if I'm sure it was stolen and not towed. They tell me to make sure. Check the tow yard. And if not, file a complaint online.

I walk the Bronx streets looking for my car. They can have the fucking thing. I just want my applications.

But come midnight I'm exhausted and alone in the Bronx, and I tell myself I can apply next year. I start laughing at the absurdity of it all. And I get on a city bus headed to Penn Station, where I can catch a train home.

*   *   *

I wake up on the couch still wearing yesterday's clothes. I wash my face in the bathroom, and when I come out I notice a manila envelope on top of the TV.

I had finished the application for Columbia and changed my mind, left it on top of the TV, because I didn't believe I was good enough to get in. I take all the materials out. The check for one hundred dollars. The letters of recommendation. It's all there.

I seal the envelope and slip on my shoes and walk the six blocks to the nearest post office. The letters have to be postmarked by today. And it's the longest of long shots, but it's the only shot I have, so I bless myself and drop it in the mailbox.

I have a long winter break, and I go to visit my mother in Arizona. She rents a small studio apartment. Police lights are swirling in the parking lot of her complex when I get there.

"What's that all about?" I ask her.

"Who knows? I think that Mexican asshole above me is running a brothel out of his apartment. I always see girls coming and going. I can't wait to get out of this shithole."

She works a lot these days.

She is saving money, has a few thousand already, wants to buy a house.

Her credit is destroyed from foreclosures and evictions.

She knows it's going to take some time.

Her eyes are bright tonight, her skin clear. She looks pretty.

In the corner a small Christmas tree is strung with lights. She asks me to help her decorate it.

"This guy I work with. He always smells like piss, but that's not the point. I was telling him about how you're in school and how you have a four-point-oh and how you met Roger Ebert. He was like, 'Wow.'"

There are a couple of boxes of ornaments that somehow survived all those moves and storage units. Every time somebody she loves dies, my mother buys a Christmas ornament to remember that person by. When she opens the first box, we see that it's full of ornaments commemorating everyone we've lost. We start hooking them onto flimsy branches. The heavier ones sag a bit. She picks up a drum-set ornament with the name CARTER engraved on it.

"Aww, Carter. You stupid ass."

She hangs it.

I take out an ornament for my father and hang it.

She hangs her sister Gina on a branch near the top.

The gold dog-biscuit ornament is for Wozels; my brother bought it for her. And I hang it.

"Aww, baby girl," she says.

My mother wipes a tear from her face.

"I was thinking about my sister Kathy the other day. The last time we spoke, I was telling her how I always wanted to buy a convertible. I've wanted one since I was a friggin' teenager."

"You should buy one," I tell her.

"I'm fifty-two years old," she says. "But that's what Kathy said—she told me to stop putting it off. Just do it. Easy for her to say. I never had the money."

She picks up another ornament.

"Maybe in another life," she says. "Wouldn't that be cool? Have the air blowing while you drive down the highway?"

I think it would be cool, too.

"So what are you studying now?"

I tell her I'm reading *The Myth of Sisyphus* by Camus.

"What's that all about?"

"It's about a guy who's been punished to a lifetime of futile labor," I tell her. "He has to push a boulder up a hill, and when he gets to the top it just rolls back down again, and he has to start all over."

"Sounds like me and this fuckin' job," she says. "Serving the same goddamn mashed potatoes every day and listening to a bunch of psychos. 'He got a bigger scoop than me!' I say, 'Shut the fuck up and make your own mashed potatoes if you don't like it.'"

"You said that?"

"I want to."

"Anyway, it's just a metaphor for the absurdity of life. Camus thinks this labor is the worst possible punishment."

"This Camus sounds like your uncle Carter. Another lazy man. I can think of worse things than futile labor. I think dying at thirty-five is worse. How about not seeing your kids grow up? That's worse."

She hangs another ornament.

"Somebody should've forced Carter to push a rock up a hill," she says. "At least he'd be alive right now. No, instead..."

She stops herself and waves me off.

"You know how fun it would be to have them all around? Now that you're all grown up? Ah, never mind. Selfish assholes. So how does this story end?"

"I think his main point is that life is absurd, and once we accept that we can find happiness in the struggle. Something like that."

She thinks for a second. "I do that with my job," she says. "I imagine myself on a beach somewhere. Drinking a piña colada on a hammock. I sit in my break room and close my eyes and pretend I can hear the waves crashing. And then some entitled bitch with three kids starts banging on my door, telling me they're hungry. I say, 'Shut the fuck up. I'm on a break.'"

Just before evening I tell her I'm going for a walk. She tells me to be careful.

I walk through familiar neighborhoods, past pink stucco roofs and trees painted white to deflect the sun. I turn onto Downing Street, where Brian and I used to ride bikes and Go-Peds and play in the orange groves and talk about wrestling and what we were going to be when we grew up. I turn onto his block, go up to his front door, and knock. He answers wearing a robe. He has a bit of a mustache and looks like an adult.

"No shit," he says, giving me a hug. "Where did you come from?"

"Home for winter break," I say.

"I heard you were in New York."

I nod.

"Nice."

I ask him how he's been.

"Better," he says. "Just got home from rehab. Cleaned up. Playing ball again. Moving to Denver."

"What's there?"

"A new start," he says. He tells me a story about waking up in a ditch on a canal after a six-day heroin bender. No idea how he got there. No idea whose clothes he was wearing.

"I was hanging out with some bad people," he says.

But he's better now.

He asks me if I still watch wrestling.

"Not as much," I say. "But I still follow it."

He asks me if I remember staying up all night and wrestling, and I say I do.

I tell him I'm happy he's doing better.

I wake up to a missed call from my brother, and a couple of texts.

> wanna go to mexico fag?
> what the fuck? answer me

I text him back:

> I can't. I have a red-eye back to new york Sunday night. Have a class Monday at 8 am.

> so come and drive ben's truck home Sunday night. Don't be a gay.

"Mom!" I yell. "Steve wants me to go to Mexico with him."
"Go ahead," she says. "Just be back in time for your flight."

The Arizona-Mexico border is congested with ugly cars blasting their horns. People are leaning out of their car windows to see what the holdup is.

We drive up to the booth, and my brother rolls down his window.

"Point of visit?"

"Pleasure."

An armed guard checks our back window using his hand as a visor and waves us on.

We drive another hour or so to Puerto Peñasco, a cheap

and dirty beach town filled with wandering lost dogs with heavy, sideways tongues hanging out of their mouths.

We wander the streets—me, my brother, and his best friend, Chris. Chris is telling me about the drug war, that he heard a news story about a local reporter who was murdered by one of the cartels when he wrote a story about a small warehouse he suspected of producing cocaine.

He tells me to be careful. "Watch out for unmarked vans. But we should be fine. Sometimes they behead American tourists," he adds. "But it's unlikely."

Our first night is spent at some nightclub on the beach. And in the morning we head to calm waters for some midday fishing with a Mexican guide.

Our unsteady boat rocks its way through the waves. I sit with Chris, our feet dangling in the water, fishing poles in our hands, the sun on the backs of our necks. The singsong creak of the boat is like a lullaby.

"Your brother says you're doing really well in school," he says.

I nod, but I don't go into it.

"That's great, dude."

He asks me how I'm doing since my dad's been gone.

"I was pretty depressed there for a while," I tell him. "My whole day was: wake up, eat a doughnut, watch TV, and go back to sleep."

"Wait a minute," he says. "That's not depression, that's retirement!"

I laugh.

"We were in Vegas not too long ago," Chris says. "Your brother and me. And there was this homeless guy. You know the type. Typical Vegas Strip scumbag. Dirty. Smells like piss and booze and cigarettes."

"But enough about you," I say and make myself laugh.

"Fuck you," he says with a laugh. "Anyway, we were outside some bar and this guy comes walking up asking for change and your brother strikes up a conversation with him. Asking all sorts of shit. Turns out he's an army vet, blah, blah, blah. Anyway, he starts talking about his daughter. She won't talk to him anymore. And your brother's like, 'Why?' He holds up his bottle of booze, goes, 'This is why,' and he takes a swig. And your brother goes, 'Well, why don't you stop?' And the guy laughs. 'Fuck her. I'll stop when I'm dead.' And your brother just fucking smashed this guy. Gets on top of this fuckin' bum and just starts beating the shit out of him. And I'm trying to pull him off, but your brother's fuckin' strong. And he's crying. And this poor guy's probably shit his pants. And Steve's pounding on him. Calling him a pussy. Crying. Screaming. And I finally get him off the guy and into the car—thankfully before the cops came.

"So he's handling it pretty well," he says and laughs.

I feel a tug on my flimsy fishing pole. It bends, and I struggle to pull it out of the water.

Chris yells that I got one.

"Reel it in!"

I pull a flopping, spastic fish out of the water. The guide grabs my pole from me.

There's a baby fish struggling at the end of the pole.

The guide says something in broken English.

"What did he say?" I ask Chris.

"When they're babies, we let them go," Chris says.

The guide removes the tiny fish from the hook and tosses him back into the ocean.

chapter 20

The ticking clock underscores the near-perfect silence of the classroom.

I'm sitting at a communal desk in front of a computer. The other students around me are still working on the quiz while my criticism professor paces with his hands behind his back.

I wait for the rest of them to finish. Check my e-mail again. Log on to Facebook. Back to my e-mail.

Refresh the page.

And there in bold black letters, an unread e-mail from the Columbia University admissions department.

The subject line says: Decision.

I click the link without thinking, before I can stop myself.

On behalf of the Admission Committee, it gives me great pleasure to inform you that you have been admitted to Columbia University.

I read the lines, but the words don't make sense in my head, so I read the message again. And again.

I stand up and walk quickly out into the hallway. I crouch down against the wall and I put my hands on my head and I feel warm tears fall down my cheeks.

And for the first time, I don't feel so invisible. I don't feel stupid today.

I exit the building and head down the sidewalk and back to the farthest building on the east side of campus and walk in the door and up the stairs and into Elizabeth's office, where she's typing at her desk.

I knock lightly and walk in. She peeks around her computer. "Hello," she says.

She can see I'm shaken up, and she seems concerned. "Everything okay?"

"Yes," I say. "I got into Columbia."

She stands and puts her hands to her face. "You got in?!"

She knew it was a Hail Mary pass. I remember sitting in her office all those weeks ago when she told me I didn't have the pedigree Columbia is looking for. She said it out of concern, not condescension, when she saw in my eyes that I had chosen to believe I could do it.

"People with stories like yours don't end up in the Ivy League," she said.

And I said, "For some reason, I think something good is going to happen."

And now she hugs me and wipes tears from her eyes.

I tell her I have to go back to class, that I'm in the middle of a quiz.

"Fuck the quiz!" she says.

* * *

I spend the summer working at *Newsday* again and finding an apartment in the Bronx. I visit Elizabeth when I feel lonely, and we chat about books and life.

When I talk about Columbia, I do it cautiously.

"You still don't believe you did it," she says. She's right. I ready myself for the moment they realized they made a mistake, the tap on my shoulder: *Mr. Porpora, we're very sorry; it's time to go home.*

And she says, "Oh, Kenny, someday I hope you'll realize how lucky they were to have you.

"Have you even told anybody yet?" she asks me, and I say my mother knows, and my brother. And Roger Ebert knows, too. I mustered the nerve to write him an e-mail, tell him he inspired me to become a writer, and thank him. He writes me back and tells me again he's always dreamed of being a graduate student and wishes me luck.

The journalism school is grand and full of gold and marble. I wear a hoodie to my classes and let it cover my eyes. I don't speak much in class, and I don't go out to the bars afterward. I do go to brunch now and then with friends I've met at school. We sit at sidewalk tables in Morningside Heights and order eggs and French toast and coffee and get to know one another. They are the smartest young people I've ever been around, and I listen to stories about their travels to impoverished nations and the places where their work has been published and their need to experience life. One girl has parents who are affluent psychiatrists, and the man next to me has a doctor for a father.

And whenever I start to feel too small to be sitting here

among them, I remember what Elizabeth said about being good enough, and I force myself to stay in my seat.

One of our breakfast meetups runs long, and as we're wrapping up I look at my phone and see MISSED CALL (7), all from my old high school friend Heather, who lives back in Arizona.

I think I know why she's calling.

I excuse myself from the table and go outside. Stand on the noisy New York sidewalk and call her back.

She answers, crying.

"Hey," I say in a soft voice. "What's up?"

And she manages to gasp out the words, "Brian died."

I take the phone from my ear for a moment, then I say, "I was worried that's why you were calling." And I tell her I'm very sorry and ask what happened.

"He hanged himself in his bedroom," she says. She breaks down all over again. "He was doing so much better."

I tell her about the last time I saw him. He looked good, said he was sober.

"Yeah, and I guess he relapsed."

I don't feel sadness. I feel anger.

That selfish fuck, I think to myself.

I walk down Manhattan Avenue as she cries to me.

I call my mother. It's still morning in Arizona.

"Hey, baby boy," she says. "I was just thinking about calling you. How's school? Hang on, let me turn the TV down. I'm watching *Regis and Kelly*. Regis is on vacation, so they got that Howie Mandel on as a guest host. If he's not a fudge packer, I don't know who is."

"School's going well," I tell her.

"Good," she says. "I gotta go back to serving sloppy joes to assholes. *C'est la vie.* It's a job. Gotta thank God for that. So what else is going on?"

"You know Brian?" I say.

"Yes."

"He died."

"He died!" she shrieks, and she immediately crumbles into tears. "Oh, that sweet boy. I'm so sorry for his family."

"I'm sorry, too," I say.

"What the fuck is wrong with these kids? Heroin at sixteen. Killing themselves! I turn the news on, and they're coming home from fucking Iraq in body bags. Jesus Christ. They should be out playing baseball. Get a hobby. Life's not that bad."

Josh Friedman, a newspaper reporter who won a Pulitzer Prize for his work about famine in Ethiopia, is my adviser for my master's thesis. He sits before a group of us wearing the expression of a friendly walrus, a warm smile below an old-fashioned mustache that swallows his upper lip. We're all discussing possible topics for our theses. The girl next to me cares more about the climate in El Salvador than I've ever seen anybody care about anything. I'm expecting blood to come pouring out of her ears as she speaks. Next to her, a Croatian woman wants to write about Chechen rebels.

And now it's my turn. And I have nothing.

Friedman pries. "You have to be an expert on something," he says. "What gets you excited? What are you passionate about?"

"Well..." I say.

He waits while I gather my thoughts.

"I do know a shitload about professional wrestling."

Everyone laughs.

Professor Friedman smiles mischievously and says he's fascinated, asks me how I got into wrestling.

"I guess my brother got me into it. And when I saw my first steel-cage match, I was hooked."

"Steel-cage match?"

I explain to the group that it's when two grown men in tights settle their differences inside the confines of a chain-link fence.

It occurs to me that professional wrestling is almost impossible to logically explain to a person who's never seen it.

"So what happened in that match?"

"It ended when one of the guys, my favorite, jumped off the side of the cage onto the other guy."

"Why would he do that?" Friedman asks.

"Oh, so he could give the other guy a big splash."

"Big splash?"

I try to think of a more serious angle. "Maybe I could follow around some wrestlers, write about steroid abuse."

"Sure," he says. "Your eyes lit up when you started talking about it. Did you ever wrestle in school? Wrestle with friends?"

Yes, I say. One friend in particular.

"Get up, Hogan!" Brian yells at me in his best Macho Man voice. He gives me an elbow smash, and I fall into the pile of blankets and pillows we've laid down on the floor.

"That's great," Friedman says. "I think we need to explore this for you."

I ask if I could be excused for a moment to use the restroom. I head down the hallway and open the bathroom door and lock it behind me.

My hands are clammy and my breath tastes bitter and I drop to my knees in front of the toilet and vomit and spit and cough and gag into the cold ceramic bowl.

I wipe the spit and vomit from my mouth and flush the toilet. I stand up and see my reflection in the mirror. My eyes are red and my face is pale and I feel so sorry for my friend.

I've spent so many years hardening my heart against addictions, so many years making fists, that I had forgotten all about the child who lives behind those dead eyes, and in those small moments when I let myself remember, when those familiar voices whisper, I am brought back to a different time, before I even knew what a monster was, and I am sad to accept that somebody who was once so kind to me, who took the time to make me feel a little bit less alone, could not find that same kindness for himself. I look into the mirror, and I'm not so sure how I wound up the lucky one, but I'm happy to be alive today.

And I say good-bye to Brian.

Our thesis meeting finishes early and I step onto the seventh-floor elevator and hit the button for the lobby when I hear, "Whoa, whoa, whoa!" and a man sticks his hand in the doors. They open back up, and he steps into the elevator next to me.

"You a student here?" he asks me. His accent sounds like he's from the Midwest. His eyes are kind.

"Yes," I say. "I'm Kenny."

"Ted," he says, and extends his hand. Ted's a visiting professor here, and he asks me if I'd like to be a part of a breaking news team who will be covering the presidential election.

I say yes, and he tells me when they're planning to meet.

* * *

On election night, Barack Obama is elected president of the United States, and Ted and I push our way through the students celebrating in the streets of Harlem, climbing on top of cars and honking horns and screaming at the top of their lungs about change. I write a few stories and watch Obama's acceptance speech on a small TV.

Just before Christmas break, I send some stories and my résumé to editors at *The New York Times,* people I've never met, strangers. I don't know how to contact them, so I guess at their e-mail addresses:

firstname.lastname@nytimes.com
firstinitiallastname@nytimes.com
lastname.firstinitial@nytimes.com

Most of the e-mails bounce back, but one makes it through to a reporter, and he writes back and asks me to come to their midtown offices for an interview. Days later I sit in a small meeting room on the forty-third floor of the New York Times Building in my secondhand suit, which needs ironing. The two editors I just finished interviewing with are deliberating down the hall. It's a long shot. The door opens. One of the men, Ian, comes in and sits and tells me he thinks I'll be a good fit. He says he wants me to join their team as a freelancer and slides a contract across the table and tosses me a pen. I sign the contract without reading it. Say thank you too many times. Promise him he won't regret it. He hands me his business card. And then he tells me to keep my phone on; they'll be in touch.

*　　*　　*

It's early January, and I'm asleep in the late afternoon when the pay-as-you-go flip phone I've dropped at least twenty times starts ringing and vibrating on my dresser. Sometimes it rings for no reason and I answer to a dial tone, frustrated, and snap it closed. I imagine it's another phantom call. *Fuck it.* I close my eyes.

The phone keeps ringing.

I grab the phone. Flip it open. On the cracked screen the number 1111111111111 is displayed.

I press the green button, expecting a dial tone.

"Hello?"

The man on the other end is already midsentence.

"We have a plane that's crashed into the Hudson River! We need you down there now! Can you go?"

"Yes!" I say. "Where?"

"Do you have a pad?"

"Yes!"

I hop around looking for a notebook. Grab an old Burger King receipt and start scribbling on the back of it. He tells me he wants me to drive down to the Hudson River and talk to everybody I can find. He wants family. He wants color. He wants details to the point of minutiae. And I'd better not fuck it up.

I hang up. Grab my shoes and socks and a wrinkled dress shirt I'd been lying on top of and throw it on.

Where the fuck are my keys?

I throw papers and pillows and crumpled jeans around until I find them in the corner.

I run out of my Bronx apartment and down the hill to the new piece-of-shit car I bought for a few hundred dollars. I see the familiar orange parking tickets sticking out from my windshield wipers. I grab the tickets and throw them onto the street. Jump into the car and speed south on the Henry Hudson Parkway.

Dusk falls over the city, and I click my headlights on. Last month I rear-ended another car while I was playing air guitar on the highway, and the right headlight still dangles lifelessly like a loose eyeball.

My phone rings again on the passenger seat.

"Hello?"

"We need you in Queens instead, at the hospital, to talk to families."

"Okay," I say. "Is everyone dead?"

"We think everybody survived," he says.

My tank is on empty, so I pull off the highway and search for a gas station.

Come on, come on. I find one and pull in and park only to get out and find my gas tank is on the other side, so I jump back in my car and pull out and make a three-point turn.

My mind is racing.

Don't fuck this up.

I run to the small Pakistani man who's eating a Snickers bar behind bulletproof glass, and I tell him I need twenty on pump nine. He pushes a metal drawer toward me and I throw my twenty-dollar bill in it and he slams it closed. I jump back in my car and speed off down the highway. I look at the tank. It's still on empty. I forgot to get the gas.

Fuck.

I cut across two lanes onto the off-ramp and turn the car around. Pound my steering wheel. Call myself a fuckup.

Pull back into the gas station and try to explain my situation to the attendant, who smiles at me.

You leave, no gas! he says, smiling wide.

I get twenty dollars' worth and floor it down the parkway. Open my phone and call my friend in Arizona.

"Gabby!"

"Everything okay?"

"Yeah. I need you to MapQuest me some directions."

She tells me she's at work, she can't right now, and I plead with her until she agrees.

George Washington Bridge to Interstate 95 for 2.7 miles.

I spend the rest of the freezing January night blowing warm air into my cupped hands outside a hospital in Queens. I ask a crying man if he knew anybody on the airplane and he asks me who I am and I say, "I'm with *The New York Times.*" I can't help but smile when I say it. He looks me over, sees my disheveled hair and my wrinkled dress clothes, the Burger King receipt I'm taking notes on, and he asks me if I'm sure.

Yes, I say. And I smile.

I interview him, ask him how he got the news, get the details, ask him if he's okay, scribble his words down. When I run out of room, I run to the reception desk and ask to borrow paper and write the rest of his story. I double-check it with him and ask if there's anybody else I can speak to. He directs me to another family, inside the hospital lobby, and I interview them, too. Women with fake nails wipe tears from their cheeks as they talk to me.

The TV news is playing behind me.

An airplane crashed into the Hudson River. The pilot saved everybody on board. Everybody survived.

They're calling it a miracle.

I call in my notes, and they tell me I can go home. It's almost midnight. My hands are purple. My heart is racing. I walk to my car. More orange parking tickets are sticking out of my windshield wipers. I pick them off and drive myself home.

The next morning the phone wakes me up again. It's my mother.

"Your name's in *The New York Times*!" she screams.

I jump out of bed, throw on my shoes, and run down to the corner store and grab a newspaper off the stack and leave two dollars on the counter. There's the plane on the front page. The headline says it was a miracle. I flip through to page A7 and scan to the bottom of the article, where a whole team of people is listed, names in italics, all the people from around the country who contributed reporting, and there, somewhere in the middle, is my name. I am one of them.

"Do you see it?" she yells through the phone. "Oh, I wish Kathy were alive to see this. She'd be so proud."

The register of her voice has changed. I can tell she's crying.

Yes, I say. I can see it.

chapter 21

In the spring semester Brian's death begins to weigh more heavily on me. My nightmares feel so real, and I start to feel the weight of all my losses at once. And the rush of New York City, the clatter of steel and the foreign tongues that flutter through midtown, which once sounded like an exotic melody to me, begins to turn sour and hiss at me. I fight loneliness on empty train cars for months before I call Ted and tell him I want to leave New York.

He tells me not to make any major decisions before we meet for coffee. We arrange to meet at the *Seinfeld* diner, which looks like the *Seinfeld* diner only from the outside. Ted orders two cups of coffee and listens.

I tell him Brian died after a struggle with drugs.

I tell him about my family.

I tell him about the first time I fell in love.

"There was a boy once," I tell him. "This blond kid in Arizona. His name was Michael. I thought I was so in love with him. He was a drug addict. He used heroin at sixteen.

Maybe even fifteen, I'm not sure. And there was just something about him."

Ted listens.

"I remember he invited me to this party once. And when I got there, he was passed out, mouth open, totally gone. And I remember looking at him and thinking he was so perfect."

He stops me.

"Listen," he says. "I am no wise man. I have made every mistake in the book. And when it comes to love, I don't know what the fuck I'm talking about. I can only share with you some of the things I've learned over the years."

He pauses and gathers his thoughts.

"Kenny, that feeling you felt when you saw that boy passed out like that . . . that feeling was not love. That is not what love feels like."

We talk about starting over. He says, "Someday you'll be surrounded by so many good people, and those darker days will be so far away.

"You're a man now, Kenny, and whatever happened happened. You can't change it. But you can choose how to live with it. We are not defined by the mistakes we make or by the number of times we fall down. Pianos will fall out of the sky. We're defined by how we respond to those challenges. And, Kenny, you have a lot of work to do on yourself. I say that because I care about you. Just like that boy you loved and your mom and your best friend all have work to do, you have work to do, too. It's just a different kind of work."

The Hofstra campus is quiet in the summer. The classrooms and parking lots and student centers are empty. I walk with my mother to the far eastern end of campus and into Elizabeth's office.

"This is my mother," I tell her, and they shake hands.

My mother says, "Kenneth has told me so much about you."

"He's told me a lot about you," Elizabeth says and hugs her.

We sit down, and Elizabeth asks about my graduation.

"It was friggin' hot out," my mother says.

I tell her it was nice. And Elizabeth says, "Your dad would've been proud."

Elizabeth hands me a graduation gift, and I open it.

It's a children's picture book called *The Three Questions.* She tells me it's based on a short story by Leo Tolstoy about a boy who sets out by himself to find the answers to three questions:

When is the best time to do things? Who is the most important one? What is the right thing to do?

She says the boy encounters a wise old turtle during his travels, and the turtle tells him, "Remember then that there is only one important time, and that time is now. The most important one is always the one you are with. And the most important thing is to do good for the one who is standing by your side." And the turtle says, "This is why we're here."

She takes my hand and tells me she wants to say something to me.

"You have come so far," she says, her voice breaking. Tears fill her dark eyes.

"It has been such an honor to work so closely with you. To watch you grow up to be a man. To watch you go to the places you've gone."

She wipes her eyes with a tissue.

And she says, "I never had any children, but if I had had a son, I would've wanted him to be just like you."

She hugs me and tells me that she loves me. And I say it back to her.

I promise her I will stay in touch, and she waves good-bye to me before my mother and I step out and I close the office door behind us.

We drive down the Long Island Expressway, heading west, toward the Midtown Tunnel, and my mother tells me a story about one of the cooks she works with who's narcoleptic. He was walking with a tray of meat loaf and just fell asleep. She's laughing and looks over at me when I don't laugh. I'm quiet and nervous in the passenger seat.

"What's wrong with you?" she asks me.

I exhale. "I want to tell you something."

"Oh, Jesus almighty. Now what? It better not be more parking tickets!"

"I'm going on a date this weekend," I tell her. "With a boy."

She looks over at me and says sharply, "You are?"

And then she's quiet for a moment. Mulls it over.

"I knew it," she says. "You always had such a crush on that Jason Timberlake."

It's quiet again between us as we drive, just the hum of passing cars, until she pipes up with more proof that she always knew.

"And you wanted to be the Wicked Witch of the West for Halloween when you were about five. I should have known then.

"*And* you asked for an Easy-Bake Oven because the

little girl across the street got one for Christmas, and you wanted one."

"Mom, I got it."

"I'm just saying."

And then she asks me, "Have you told your brother?"

I tell her I haven't.

When I call my brother in Flagstaff, he tells me he's at the gym and can't talk.

"It's important," I tell him.

"Fine. What? I have five minutes."

"I'm going on a date this weekend, with a boy."

"I know. Mommy told me."

"She told you?"

"Of course she did. You're so dramatic, by the way."

"What did she say?"

"She said she doesn't think you're gay, she thinks you're just bored."

I laugh.

"Did she freak out when you told her?" he asks me.

"No," I say. "She was actually pretty cool about it."

"Well, that's good," he says. "So what does this mean? Are you going to start wearing boas and heels everywhere?"

I tell him it does.

"You better hook me up with some of your hot girlfriends."

"I will."

He tells me he has to get back to the gym, but he'll call me later.

Corinne Novella is a social worker at the Washington Square Institute, and though she's only in her late twenties she's dressed like a school counselor. We sit in her office, which is small and lit by a single desk lamp, and she stares at me, waiting for me to talk.

"Am I supposed to start?" I ask her.

It's our third session, and I still haven't gotten the hang of therapy.

She doesn't speak, just tilts her head a bit to one side.

"I'm here because I had a professor who told me I had some work to do on myself. My friend killed himself last year. And it sort of broke open the dams, the levees, and, like I told you last time, I've been crying a lot."

She's nodding.

"I remember that when he first started using I used to have these fantasies of saving him. Like, he'd see that I would stick by him through anything, and, I don't know, he'd love me in return. But they've never loved me more than they've loved that fucking drug. Or the vodka. Whatever it is."

"Who are 'they'?"

"I don't know," I say. "Everybody."

I look away from her.

"I have felt like an old man my whole life. And they get to have fun and snort their fucking drugs and get wasted and it doesn't matter who they're hurting because they're young and having fun and *I'm* a judgmental prick if I say anything."

"Do you think they're having fun?"

I don't have an answer for her.

"I'll never be able to compete against it."

"Maybe you don't understand how powerful it is," she says.

"How powerful is it?"

"Very."

"And that's an excuse?"

"No."

"When do they get to take responsibility?"

"For themselves?" she asks.

"Yes."

"Always," she says.

It's in our next session that we talk about anger.

"You're holding back," she says.

"When Brian died I wasn't sad," I tell her. "I was mad. And I stayed mad for a long time. I didn't even go to his funeral."

"Why were you angry?"

I take a moment. "He knew what was going to happen. You know, I almost felt vindicated when I heard he was dead. Like his death made me feel like I had made the right choices with my life. Like I knew that shit would lead to death, and nobody would listen to me. So now he's dead."

She asks me if I'm ashamed to feel that way, and I say yes.

"They always act like they're not hurting anybody but themselves, but that isn't true."

"You keep saying 'they.' Who are you really angry at?"

"What do you want me to say? My mother?"

"Are you angry at your mother?"

"She was the most thoughtful person I have ever known," I tell her. "She could meet you once and remember your birthday forever. She'd send you Easter baskets. She'd do anything to make you feel loved."

I am quiet.

"And she was the nastiest drunk I've ever met."

I am quiet again.

"Sometimes I think, Was she thinking about me when she was drinking? Did any of them ever think about me when they were putting straws in their noses and needles in their arms? Did they even think about me once?"

And she asks me, "What would it mean if they didn't?"

I stare at her, trembling. She knows what I think it means, and she wants me to say it out loud.

I let the time run out on our session. Before I go she asks me if I've ever thought about writing about my life. I tell her I haven't. She says it might help. Might bring some clarity, some peace. I thank her. Tell her I'll see her again next week.

My first job after school is writing about the Yankees for the New York *Daily News*.

"Don't think I'm rooting for those motherfuckers just because you're writing about them," my mother says. "Go, Mets!"

When the baseball season ends, I cover the John Gotti Jr. trial for the *Daily News*. The jury is stalled for days, and I have lunch every day at a table across from Victoria Gotti and her lawyer and her family and other reporters inside the courthouse cafeteria. On the day the jury calls it quits and a mistrial is declared, I end up outside Gotti's mother's house, and she invites us in for pasta and meatballs and red gravy. I politely turn her down.

Late that night, on the sidewalk outside her house, I'm talking to my cameraman, telling him I got a job offer in California as an editor for a news website.

"LA?"

"San Francisco," I tell him.

"You going to do it?" he asks me, and before I can answer he starts ranting about how sick he is of paying New York City taxes and Long Island's worse and fuck that *sonofabitch*

Bloomberg and don't even get him started on snow shoveling in the winter.

I tell him I'm thinking about it.

"San Francisco!" he says with a sigh. "Great town. I was out there when I was around your age. Six months of brunch and anal sex. You like acid?"

My plane lands at SFO in May.

I take a Caltrain up north into the city and hop off into the middle of downtown skyscrapers. It looks a little like New York. But it's different. There are no ghosts out here. The sky is bright blue, and the clouds are lighter. And it's a place of my own, where I can make new memories that are all mine. I work and make friends and on the weekends we dance and run around the city and take photographs and do the kinds of things I always imagined people my age do. Now and then I see a balloon caught in the power lines, holding on, waving, flapping softly in the evening air, and I wonder if somebody in some faraway city tried to send it to heaven the way my mother and I used to do.

I close my laptop after a morning of writing in a coffee shop and put the computer in my backpack. I head out of the café and walk down 24th Street, past its flower shops and bakeries and bookstores, and turn up a steep hill, then another, taking long strides to the top, and turn to face the steepest of them, struggling the whole way up, and pause when I reach the top, hands on my knees to catch my breath. I can see the whole city from way up here. The hills in the distance. The settled fog by the bay. All the colors and the lights and the waving flags and the bluest water, which seems to go on forever.

It's a beautiful day way up here. And I let myself have the moment, try to hold it in my memory, before I walk down the hill through the side streets and into the city, where young parents push strollers and steel buildings soar like spotlights into the sky, and I get myself lost in the crowd of tourists and beggars and street performers. Then I push on, walking at a daydreamer's pace as afternoon turns into evening, thinking about what a pretty word *tomorrow* can be.

And if it turns out I'm going the wrong way home, then so be it.

It's a nice night to get lost.

Never mind the hills.

acknowledgments

Many small families were created to bring this story of a very fractured one to light: It started with my agent Jeff Kleinman, who believed with passion from the first word, and my editor Emily Griffin, whose thoughtfulness transformed these words into an actual book. Years ago, when I'd daydream of being a writer, it wasn't accolades or success I'd dream of; it was working with people like you, and I feel lucky and privileged to have done so. Thank you for your patience, your creativity, and your support. I'll never forget that.

I was so fortunate to work with so many amazing people at Grand Central Publishing: Thank you to Carolyn Kurek and Barbara Clark for reading this book with such an attuned eye to detail and accuracy; to Lisa Rivlin for being so mindful of those closest to me; to Anne Twomey for her overwhelming enthusiasm for the book and for turning that enthusiasm into the stunning book cover that helped bring this story to life; and to Jamie Raab for standing behind us all with an unwavering support. Working so closely with you all has been one of the highlights of my life.

There were many writers who took the time to help me out even though I was a mere stranger: Poe Ballantine, that fearless writer and essayist who answered my very random e-mail asking him for help, and who took the time to read a chapter of an early draft. Poe, your encouragement and honesty helped me in ways you may never know. Thank you to Andre Dubus III for endorsing the book with such love and enthusiasm. Andre, I am touched and overwhelmed by your support. Thank you to Lee Martin for doing the same, and for extending your friendship when I most needed it. A special thank you is needed for Lidia Yuknavitch, Junot Diaz, George Saunders, Dave Eggers, and Adam Haslett, all of whom have taken the time to extend a hand to me at some point during this process. Just knowing you were all out there helped get me through this.

Thank you to Elizabeth Unruh for always believing and for never going easy on me; thank you to Joe Cutbirth for the advice, the stories, and the friendship; thank you to Roger Ebert for giving me words to live my life by; thank you to the poet Stephen Dunn for teaching me how to be an honest man; and thank you to Isaac Wade, the only person I trust to read my writing, for seeing something when nobody else did.

I would like to thank my closest friends Gabrielle Walz, Chris Warnack, Claire Moses, Maija Sjogren, and Heather Sullivan for all the years of real friendship.

To the members of my family who are no longer with us, I'd like to say I'm sorry. There is a quote by Stephen Dunn I've always loved; he says, "Our parents died at least twice, the second time when we forgot their stories." I hope by remembering your stories, the good and the bad, you can forgive me for sharing parts of your lives you may have wished to have kept private. Most of all I'd like to thank my father, whom I think would've been proud of this story. And I'd like to thank Joy Wozels for teaching me about friendship and loyalty and love.

And to my family, to my mother and brother, thank you for allowing me to tell this story. Thank you for living it with me and for surviving it with me. I know sometimes words fall short, but I hope these words come close to expressing how important you both are to me.

about the author

KENNY PORPORA has written for *The New York Times*, the New York *Daily News*, and *Newsday*. He is a graduate of Columbia University's School of Journalism and Hofstra University. *The Autumn Balloon* is his first book.